Dear Ray,
Sending you a numbered &
signed copy (only 500!) with
much love — your name comes
up in one of the chapters!
Chloe    August 2007

QUANTUM CHANGE MADE EASY

A RESONANCE REPATTERNING BOOK

~~~

# QUANTUM CHANGE MADE EASY

~~~

*Breakthroughs in Personal Transformation,*
*Self-Healing and Achieving the*
*Best of Who You Are*

## CHLOE FAITH WORDSWORTH

Founder of the Resonance Repatterning® System

### with Gail Noble Glanville

RESONANCE PUBLISHING
Scottsdale, Arizona

A RESONANCE REPATTERNING BOOK

**Quantum Change Made Easy:**
Breakthroughs in Personal Transformation, Self-Healing
and Achieving the Best of Who You Are

© 2007 Chloe Faith Wordsworth

*Published by:*
Resonance Publishing, a division of
Resonance Repatterning Institute, LLC
PO Box 4578, Scottsdale, Arizona 85261–4578 USA
www.ResonanceRepatterning.net
info@ResonanceRepatterning.net

Photographs from *Cymatics: A Study of Wave Phenomena and Vibration* by
Hans Jenny © 2001 MACROmedia Publishing. Used by permission.
www.cymaticsource.com

First Edition 2007

14 13 12 11 10 09 08 07    8 7 6 5 4 3 2 1    III II I
ISBN 978-0-9794334-0-5

Library of Congress Control Number: 2007923337

Cover design by George Foster — www.fostercovers.com
Book design and composition by Valerie Brewster, Scribe Typography
Printed in the USA with soy ink on paper made from both recycled papers
and trees grown in sustainable forests.

*To the Friend*
*with gratitude*

# CONTENTS

# FOREWORD

It is a privilege to write a Foreword for a book that will help many of us experience better health and more rewarding lives. Chloe Wordsworth has discovered Nine Keys that can unlock the doors to the psyche, to allow the emergence of new and regenerated individuals. Here she details her approach and gives readers practical techniques they can use to enrich and empower their lives. Experience shows that the beneficial results of this work are contagious, spreading to families, friends, business associates and even to larger organizations.

Through this work, many people have identified and transformed outdated life patterns that created recurring problems. Sometimes these are simply repetitive stories one tells oneself again and again. It is always a challenge to undo old habits, especially if we do not recognize they are there. We all have inner patterns that keep us constricted and even resistant to positive change. All of these issues limit our experience of life and may also disturb those around us. When you recognize your story and its origins, you will see your problems from a new perspective. What could be more exciting than a method that can deliver us, individually and collectively, from the recurring effects of our past traumas and make life easier and more fun?

There is no work more significant for these times. For at every level and in every direction we sense small or large issues that prevent all of us from living in the world of peace and happiness that everyone longs for.

Resonance Repatterning is a practical system based on three interrelated principles of physics: quantum mechanics, coherence and resonance. Let us take a brief look at these phenomena and their significance for a healthy and successful life.

The "quantum leap" was born on December 14, 1900, at a meeting of the German Physical Society. Max Planck presented his discovery that the amount of energy in an object that is being heated does not increase smoothly, but increases in discrete steps or quantum jumps, with no intermediate levels. This was the birth of quantum mechanics, one of the most successful theories in the history of science. It turned out that quantum leaps are a built-in property of the entire universe. For more than a century since Planck's revelations, quantum theory has expanded physics and technology far beyond their classical limits, and has also produced some of the most challenging paradoxes of the human mind.

The "quantum leap" is familiar to every energy therapist. A patient, whose life has long been held hostage by a concept or by a traumatic memory, suddenly recognizes the truth behind a health or relationship issue. In an instant of vivid clarity, a breathtaking physical and/or emotional transformation takes place. The effect is system-wide. Every cell in the body is affected. The future is suddenly much brighter.

One of the great discoveries that followed from quantum physics is that when atoms or molecules are energized, they can vibrate in unison and emit coherent energy such as that produced by a laser. Biological coherence[1] is the description of the way the atoms and molecules in the body can come into physical and energetic alignment with each other. It is a whole-body phenomenon involving all of the tissues, not just the nervous system.

The process of creating biological coherence is greatly enhanced when traumatic scars and holding patterns have been resolved, a process that takes place with the Resonance

Repatterning system. The quantum leap is thus describable in terms of an energetic radiance that can be seen or felt by those in the vicinity of the individual undergoing the transformation.

The vibrant alignment of one's molecules creates far more than health. Through the connections of your body with the vast fabric of space, the world around you begins to align with your purpose or destiny. The physics of the situation is much like that of the ripples that go out when you throw a pebble into a pond of water. Love, appreciation, confidence, self-worth and hope are all coherent states of being that are radiated into the space around you and that make it easier for others to shift in the same direction. Your actions and your words become more coherent, awareness increases, and even your sense of humor may be enhanced. When we are chaotic, it is difficult to manifest our intentions; when we are coherent the universe supports us.

There is a science that describes these quantum leaps. They are referred to as cooperative or collective or synergetic phenomena, in which the parts of an organism or its psyche self-organize in response to a tiny stimulus. Physical and/or emotional order can suddenly emerge from chaos; new and surprisingly wonderful behaviors can arise—properties that cannot be predicted on the basis of the study of the parts.

Biological systems are non-linear. The science of non-linear phenomena emerged from the work of Ilya Prigogine, who received the Nobel Prize in 1977. The significance of linear/non-linear phenomena is that with a linear system, the more energy you put into it, the bigger the change produced. Non-linear systems are not like this. A tiny input of energy into a living system can lead to a huge change. Resonance Repatterning displays a sophisticated understanding of the ways subtle influences can bring about large shifts.

It is the task of the scientist to make visible or logical those aspects of nature that normally cannot be seen. Resonance is such a phenomenon. Every object in the universe, from the smallest to the largest, has a natural frequency that it will emit when it vibrates. The "tuning fork effect" is a classic example of resonance. It is the mechanism by which atoms, molecules and other objects can interact with each other without touching. It is the mechanism by which coherence and good feelings entrain the frequencies of those around you.

I have demonstrated the tuning fork effect in workshops. I use two tuning forks resonant at 440 cycles per second, corresponding to the musical note A above middle C. This is the standard musical pitch for tuning musical instruments and orchestras. Before a concert, the concertmaster signals to the oboist to play an A for the wind instruments. Then he tunes his violin to that same A and plays it for the strings. In the end, the entire orchestra tunes to the same 440 A.

I strike one of my tuning forks and immediately it vibrates. I place its base against the table, which acts as a sounding board, and everyone can hear the tone. The other tuning fork is mounted on a microphone connected to an audio amplifier and loudspeaker. I bring the first tuning fork, which is emitting a tone of 440 cycles per second, close to the second tuning fork. The second fork picks up the vibrations from the first (they resonate) and it produces the same tone, which is detected and amplified so everyone can hear it. This is resonance, or the transfer of a vibration between two objects with the same natural frequency.

In the tuning fork effect, the vibration is carried through air. Resonance can also take place with electromagnetic vibrations conducted through space. This is the basis for radio and television. A transmitter creates an oscillating or vibrating electromagnetic field that carries a signal through space to a receiver tuned to the same frequency, many miles away.

We used to think of space as "empty." This is no longer the case. Physicists have realized that even a total vacuum is a very busy place, bubbling with the strands of energy and information that connect all objects with all other objects. This "quantum foam" surrounds us and penetrates into every nook and cranny of our bodies.

The remarkable power of resonance was dramatically demonstrated during the space program. Pioneer 10 was the first manmade object to leave the solar system. On the 30th anniversary of its launch, NASA sent a radio message to the spacecraft, which was then 7.4 billion miles away. The message was sent from a radio telescope in the desert east of Los Angeles, and a radio telescope in Spain received a response from the spacecraft 22 hours and six minutes later. Pioneer's transmitter has a power of 40 watts, comparable to a small light bulb.[2]

This astonishing example tells me that resonance is real and that it can act across billions of miles beyond our solar system. Is it a surprise, then, that the coherence produced by Resonance Repatterning can influence family members and others in close relationship to the recipient? Is it a surprise that Resonance Repatterning can be done at a distance, over the telephone, for example? If resonance can act across 7.6 billion miles of space, it should also act across a few miles separating a Resonance Repatterning practitioner and the client they are talking to on the telephone. And it does.

This is one of the challenging paradoxes of quantum mechanics. We learn at an early age that we are individuals, with thoughts and feelings separate from those of the others around us. What quantum mechanics teaches is that this is actually an illusion; that all objects in the universe are continuously interconnected through a vast webwork of interacting quantum fields, referred to as the quantum vacuum or the unifying field. This field is organized like a hologram, with each part containing information on the whole. As Chloe points out, "Creating order in just one part automatically benefits the whole."

What I especially admire in this work of Resonance Repatterning is the generous way all modalities are treated. Chloe has studied virtually every approach to healing, every therapeutic school. All are valued and recommended where appropriate. Resonance Repatterning practitioners have no vested interest in promoting one form of therapy over another. Instead, they identify the treatment that is most needed for the individual at the present moment. There is no hesitation to send the person to an acupuncturist, polarity therapist, physician or whatever. For many, this means the end of a long search for the solution to their health or relationship problems.

The ability to locate the best way to proceed with a patient involves a special kind of deep listening, for people are different and there is no method that works with everyone. One result of this is that one feels deeply touched and listened to. And the accuracy of the listening is verified by using a sophisticated measuring technique involving a new version of Applied Kinesiology.

Much wisdom has emerged from this work. One piece is a deeper understanding of the meaning of our "problems" and how they present opportunities for change. This is Repatterning in action. It involves tuning in to the invisible world of the unconscious. Since the most relevant phenomena are often beyond verbal discussion, special techniques are needed to reach them. As energy begins to flow, debris and blockages are swept aside, allowing for greater flow, which further unblocks the system. New pathways open, leading to new possibilities.

This is a perfect book for the person contemplating entering the healing field, and will also inspire all who are already well versed in specific modalities. I have long held that it is only through work of this type that humankind can awaken to the possibilities that lie before us and resonate coherently with the creative steps needed to avoid the pitfalls lying on the other side of our potential.

James L. Oschman, PhD
Author of *Energy Medicine: The Scientific Basis* and
*Energy Medicine in Therapeutics and Human Performance*

---

1. H. Fröhlich, editor. "Biological Coherence and Response to External Stimuli." Berlin: Springer Verlag, 1988.

2. *USA Today:* Monday, March 4, 2002, p. 3A.

# PROLOGUE

*Health is a state of complete physical, mental and social well-being
and not merely the absence of disease and infirmity.*

WORLD HEALTH ORGANIZATION

When I was eight years old, I wouldn't go to sleep at night unless I had my favorite book, *The Living Touch,* under my pillow. A small book on healing by Dorothy Kerin, it struck a deep chord within me. Night after night, I longed to be a healer like her.

Many years later, I read a story by Richard Selzer about Yeshi Dhonden, physician to the Dalai Lama, who had been invited to make rounds at the hospital where Dr. Selzer worked. Dr. Selzer's story hints at the quality of presence and the healing touch Yeshi Dhonden possessed, which changed Dr. Selzer's life as a doctor. Like Dorothy Kerin's book, this story has continued to move and inspire me in my own life work.

Dr. Selzer describes the early morning rounds when a group of curious Western doctors gathered to meet the Tibetan monk and physician. Yeshi Dhonden, it was explained, would examine a patient whose diagnosis was unknown to him, as it was to all the doctors present except for the patient's own doctor, who was hosting the rounds.

On entering the patient's room, Yeshi Dhonden, without speaking, gazed for a long time at a point above where the woman lay. Finally he took her hand, and for half an hour "listened" in silence to the pulses that told him the secrets of her sickness. Dr. Selzer, standing at the foot of the woman's bed, describes his feelings:

> All at once I am envious—not of him, not of Yeshi

Dhonden for his gift of beauty and holiness, but of her. I want to be held like that, touched so, received. And I know that I, who have palpated a hundred thousand pulses, have not felt a single one.

No words were exchanged, yet as Yeshi Dhonden turned to leave, the woman called to him "Thank you, doctor," in a voice both urgent and serene.

"Thank you, doctor." Yeshi Dhonden asked no questions. He didn't attempt to cure her. He listened to the murmurings of her body and later provided a complete diagnosis that matched exactly what her attending physician knew. "The last spendings of an imperfect heart," Yeshi Dhonden said. "Congenital heart disease," her doctor confirmed.

Yeshi Dhonden's presence, the seed of his being, nurtured both the woman and the watching physicians. The truth is that the longing to be "touched"—to be listened to by someone who receives the truth held in our body and mind—is universal. More than fifty-five years after insisting that *The Living Touch* be part of my sleeping world, I recognize with gratitude the times when I have been touched by something sacred; the times when a generous listening presence has helped me connect to the seed of my being.

## Foundations

For the last thirty-five years, health and healing have been the focus of my work with others. I have been fortunate to study with people who know the secret of the living touch. In my twenties, I remember listening to Dr. Randolph Stone, the founder of Polarity Therapy, as he inspired and confused me by turns. Though eighty-four years old, he would end a long day of teaching by seeing patients until late into the night. What I remember most about him was his profound compassion.

One evening I was relaxing for a few minutes in the garden when Dr. Stone came out for a breath of fresh air. Suddenly he looked at me with intensity; waving his finger at me, he said: "This has been a revelation for you!" Without another word, he turned and went back into the house. I knew that he was saying something important. Only later did I realize that the revelation came from the understanding of the body-mind energy field he opened to me and from the quality of who he was as a person. It was this experience with Dr. Stone that initiated me into the field of energy medicine.

Years later I studied Five Element Acupuncture. In my clinical work with Professor J. R. Worsley, I was again reminded that healing includes and goes beyond the cure of the physical body. About to enter a room where a patient was waiting for his diagnosis, JR, as we called him, suddenly stopped with his hand on the doorknob. In that moment of stillness, I felt he was leaving his personality, his small self, behind. When he entered the patient's room he was tangibly changed: he embodied the compassionate presence that he brought to all the clients he saw.

During my years of searching for answers in the complementary healthcare field—studying, learning, reading, practicing, teaching—I was always looking, unsuccessfully I felt, for ways to deeply touch another person. How could I receive the truth I knew was there but that we seldom access? I wanted a practical way to identify and transform whatever it was that creates our recurring problems. I wanted to teach a system that would empower people to help themselves, so they could "touch" and "be touched." Knowledge of energy and healing modalities was not enough. I was looking for something more.

Like many practitioners in the complementary healthcare

field, I questioned why the same technique is successful with one person and not with another. I wondered why we repeat the same emotional turmoil and toxic relationships, and most of all why we keep ourselves so small when our divine nature is so infinitely great.

## Common ground

Fortunately we live in an extraordinary era in which physics, kinesiology, psychology and neurobiology are finding common ground with the ancient knowledge and healing wisdom of India and China. With combined insights from these fields, I found new ways to help my clients create positive change in their life and their health.

The first insight came from the development of Applied Kinesiology, also known as muscle testing. Through this system, practitioners put pressure on a muscle and observe its strong/relaxed response to obtain information on the flow of energy through the human body.

In the 1970s I began to use this tool to identify the best health or healing modality for my clients. Rather than use a modality dictated only by my diagnostic training, I would muscle check to ascertain the modality best suited for balancing the client's body-mind system. Over time, I found myself using muscle testing in ways that were new to the field of Applied Kinesiology and eventually renamed my theory-based application *Resonance Kinesiology* and *muscle checking.*

A second insight came from the field of physics: the concept of resonance. I discovered that people "resonate" with certain patterns, habits, or ways of perceiving their lives. This was true whether those patterns were healthy for them or not. I learned

that through their resonance with their deeply grooved neuro-
logical, psychological and energy frequency patterns, they were
locked into a life that was often painful—including addictions,
poor choices in relationships and careers, and unhealthy diets.
From my clinical observations, I wrote down these unconscious
energy patterns and noted how they could be transformed into
what I called "coherent" patterns.

As my clients changed their resonance from *life-inhibiting*
patterns and resonated instead with *life-expanding* patterns, they
felt liberated from the negative, usually unconscious attitudes
that had run their lives. More importantly, they felt touched and
deeply listened to. The positive outcomes that resulted—physically, emotionally and mentally—went far beyond my highest
expectations.

## Evolution of a system

Resonance Kinesiology was the missing piece—a way for any
trained practitioner to listen deeply to the truth the body-mind
holds. My eureka moment came when I realized that frequencies, patterns, the new system of muscle checking and all the
modalities I had learned, were the "listening touch" I had
longed for. I called this new system Holographic Repatterning®
—now known as the Resonance Repatterning® system.

Based on insights from modern physics, psychology and
ancient healing traditions, the Resonance Repatterning system
is a practical application of the following principles:

- All matter consists of pulsing frequencies of energy.

- We are energy beings living in an ocean of vibrating
  frequencies—the unified field.

- The quality of our life depends on the quality of the frequencies we resonate with.

- When we resonate with more beneficial, coherent frequencies, we naturally change ourselves, our attitudes and our experience of life for the better.

- We always have a point of choice to resonate with what is non-coherent and de-energizing or to resonate with what is coherent and life-enhancing.

Applying these principles in the laboratory of my full-time private practice, I saw consistent and often extraordinary results. Many clients, impressed by their personal experience, began asking how they might learn to do what I was doing. My work was deeply ingrained. I had a structure in my head for what I was doing, which I freely adapted in the moment to suit each client's needs. To put it on paper was a whole new challenge.

In the early 1990s I began to write the training manuals and develop a method of teaching the system so almost anyone, regardless of age or background, could learn it. The intention of the training manuals is to enable people to identify the limiting patterns they resonate with and to easily facilitate a change in resonance both for themselves and others.

During the last fifteen years, the Resonance Repatterning system has spread by word of mouth to countries around the world. The Resonance Repatterning Institute, responding to the growing needs of students and practitioners, now includes standards-based training for people who want to apply this work in their personal lives and in working with others; commercial trademark licensing for use of the name, logo and repatterning manuals; and a creative, high-standard teacher training. There is also an independent, non-profit membership association that offers peer-reviewed professional certification of practitioners.

**The Nine Keys**

*Quantum Change Made Easy* introduces you to the Nine Keys that Resonance Repatterning students, practitioners and teachers use on themselves and with others. The Keys, listed below, are interrelated and work together to help practitioners of the Resonance Repatterning system create greater health, happiness and harmony for themselves and others.

## 1: ENERGY

*Everything is energy. Energy is everything.*

## 2: RESONANCE

*Change your resonance, change your life.*

## 3: KINESTHETICS

*You are wired for coherence and self-healing.*

## 4: ORIENTATION

*Oriented, you face the direction that nurtures your soul.*

## 5: PROBLEMS

*Underneath every problem is an empowering truth.*

## 6: INTENTION

*All great outcomes begin with intention.*

## 7: REPATTERNING

*Bring your hidden patterns to light.*

## 8: MODALITIES

*Modalities harmonize and balance the flow of energy.*

## 9: ACTION

*Every coherent action leads to more coherence.*

Each chapter on the Nine Keys ends with a guided activity that gives you a taste of the Resonance Repatterning system. These activities may help you neutralize your resonance with a problem and boost your resonance with new coherent patterns. When you complete the activities, you may feel less stressed out or emotionally charged; the repetitive stories you tell yourself may change; you might find yourself seeing a problem from a different perspective. If you would like a deeper and more complete experience of Resonance Repatterning, you are welcome to have a session with a Certified Practitioner.

### Words we use

Some of the words in this book may be new to you. Some of the terms describe contemporary concepts from physics that are now more widely recognized and are being applied in a practical way. Other words come from ancient wisdom traditions that have been generally unknown in the West but are now increasingly respected by those exploring the fields of consciousness and science. You will find all these words defined in the glossary, "Words We Use," at the end of the book.

### Our personal and shared humanity

This book deliberately uses both the "we" and the "you" voice.

The "we" voice refers to our general, shared humanity. It is inclusive and broad. It may or may not speak to us personally. The "you" voice addresses you personally. It asks you to look at yourself directly, to consider how the information applies to you, your relationships and your life.

## Stories, confidentiality and resonance

I have included stories from and about people who have benefited over the years from sessions, seminars and the use of the Nine Keys. Other stories were shared by clients, and by certified Resonance Repatterning practitioners and teachers. The names and sufficient details of all the case histories have been changed to protect the identity of those concerned and the confidential nature of the sessions.

I've often chosen stories that are dramatic in nature to illustrate the range of benefits that result from Resonance Repatterning sessions. Some clients may have immediate and often dramatic results similar to the sessions described in this book; other clients may not.

My experience is that in every session there is always a measurable change in resonance. When the change in resonance occurs at the quantum level, results may not be dramatically visible. Whereas when the change in resonance occurs at the frequency level of the body, emotions and mind, the results may be more obvious. Sometimes change happens quickly and sometimes it takes place over time. In every case, however, the muscle checking tool confirms the precise changes in resonance that take place in these sessions, and the client can actually see and feel the change through their own muscle response.

The purpose of Resonance Repatterning is to facilitate a change in resonance. Nature—the body-mind field—can then create balance. Many people like to have sessions simply to support their on-going process for maintaining balance and growth, and their physical, mental and social well-being.

## Your self-healing

If you feel stuck or triggered at any point as you read these pages, I encourage you to stop, take a deep breath and use the *Action* steps in the box at the end of the chapter you are reading. You may be surprised at how powerful these small tools are for re-establishing a sense of balance and well-being. You may realize that you became stuck for a reason and that you are ready to benefit from the practices offered at the end of the chapter or from a practitioner who can more specifically access the place asking for self-healing.

~~~~

In *Quantum Change Made Easy,* I am happy to introduce the principles I teach and use every day. For me, they are Keys that open the door to hope, inspiration, self-healing and growth. I offer them to you as a way to enhance your life, change a negative state of mind, and create a new way of living and relating. You may enjoy using these Keys daily for yourself, your family and friends, your clients and colleagues—and, because we are all holographically connected through frequencies in the unified field, you will help improve the world we all share.

~~~

# THE NINE KEYS

~~~

*The Nine Keys are much more than individual steps.*

*When put together in a synergistic system,*

*they provide an empowering and beneficial way*

*to bring order to your life*

*and help you manifest your potential.*

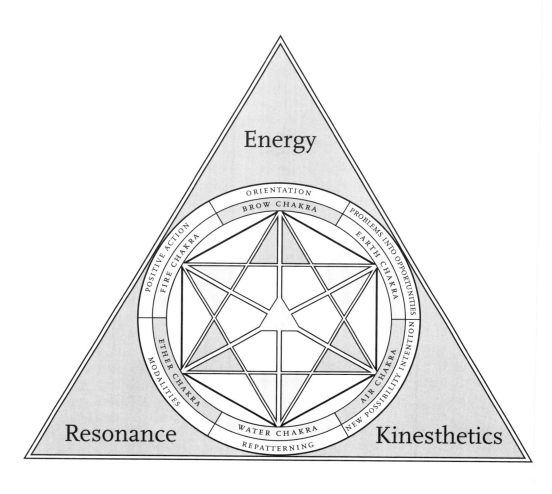

Energy

Resonance

Kinesthetics

ORIENTATION

BROW CHAKRA

PROBLEMS INTO OPPORTUNITIES

POSITIVE ACTION

FIRE CHAKRA

EARTH CHAKRA

ETHER CHAKRA

MODALITIES

AIR CHAKRA

NEW POSSIBILITY INTENTION

WATER CHAKRA

REPATTERNING

# THE NINE KEYS

~~~~~

*When you change the way you look at things,*

*the things you look at change.*

MAX PLANCK

A friend told me about meeting with a small group of business people in their private club. They were curious to learn about the field of quantum energy in which we live, so she introduced them to the fundamental principles of Resonance Repatterning. Since they were in a seaside community, she included the cosmic question by a student droplet who asks the philosopher droplet: "So what's this ocean you're always talking about?"

At one point in her talk, one of the men interrupted her to say: "I appreciate the principles you describe. I've read books about the power of my mind and creating my own reality. I just don't know how to actually put it to use, especially to benefit my business."

I agree with this businessman. It is one thing to learn scientific principles about the ocean of frequencies in which we exist and yet know nothing about; it's quite another thing to know how to apply them in a practical way. It can seem impossible, even with inspired self-help books and therapy, to undo habits such as the need to be right or being overly reactive. Like everyone else, you might have a great deal of inner patterning or imprinting that keeps you constricted, limited and even resistant to positive change. Too many people feel locked up from the inside without a key, unable to free themselves from the pain and limitation they suffer, or from the suffering they impose on others—often the people they love the most.

Positive change requires a structured system for gently opening the door to resonate with your true strengths and gifts. This book describes such a structured system: the nine fundamental Keys on which the Resonance Repatterning system is based. By reading the book and doing the activities at the end of each chapter, you will discover something new about yourself, and you will see how to actually put the basic principles of the Nine Keys to use in your own life, in a practical way.

## The Keys

The first three of the Nine Keys—Energy, Resonance and Kinesthetics—reveal the beauty and potential of the invisible world of energy within each one of us. This is the inner world of vibrating frequencies through which we know the truth of what supports our life and what doesn't.

The next four Keys are like a prism: Orientation, Problems, Intention and Repatterning. Each facet of the prism reveals a different way to see and transform the resonance that limits us. Each one of these Keys will show you a different way to change your resonance with disorientation, resistance to problems, the projections that block intention, and non-coherent patterns of energy. Through these four Keys, you will also be able to identify the new patterns that will support your upward spiral to well-being, better health and fulfilling relationships.

The last two keys are Modalities and Positive Action. When you select and implement a modality, which is a highly coherent frequency, negative frequency patterns are neutralized and positive frequency patterns are amplified. Then through coherent actions you resonate with, you are able to sustain your new patterns and potentially send ripples across the entire spectrum of human consciousness.

## The Mandala

You can see that the Mandala and triangle illustration at the beginning of each chapter is a picture of the Nine Keys, and the complete methodology for creating quantum change. At the center of the Mandala, the tetrahedron represents body, emotions and mind. The three-dimensional point of the tetrahedron represents spirit, or consciousness. All the lines of the Mandala converge at this central point—the pivotal hub where quantum change is initiated.

## Coherence Continuum

The spiral illustration on the next page is a continuum of noncoherent and coherent frequencies. If you have spiraled down into non-coherence in any area of your life, you have the power to recognize your point of choice to stay where you are, or to spiral up. When you make the decision to spiral up, you become receptive to spirit, or consciousness. You embark on the life journey of changing the patterns you resonate with and thereby live in a higher state of coherence.

~~~

## Coherence Continuum

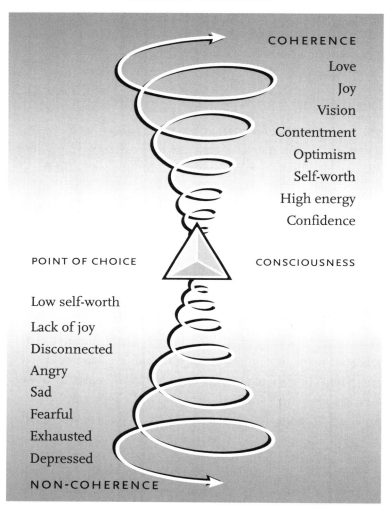

COHERENCE

Love

Joy

Vision

Contentment

Optimism

Self-worth

High energy

Confidence

POINT OF CHOICE

CONSCIOUSNESS

Low self-worth

Lack of joy

Disconnected

Angry

Sad

Fearful

Exhausted

Depressed

NON-COHERENCE

# KEY 1

~~~

# THE ENERGY OF LIFE

~~~

*Everything is energy.*

*We live in an ocean of vibrating frequencies,*

*organized as a hologram*

*in which each part contains the whole.*

*Creating order in just one part*

*automatically benefits the whole.*

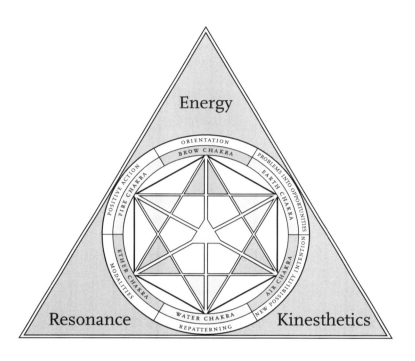

ENERGY
RESONANCE
KINESTHETICS
ORIENTATION
PROBLEMS
INTENTIONS
REPATTERNING
MODALITIES
ACTION

# KEY 1

~~~

*Everything is energy. Energy is everything.*

Imagine your life energy as water flowing through a hose. When your life is positive, events flow with harmony and your life energy moves in ways that give you a sense of well-being. When a disturbing incident happens—like an argument, accident, or loss of some kind—your energy constricts in response. It's as though someone has put their foot on your hose, depressing it so the flow is reduced to a trickle. You may even feel that the problem, or the person involved with any problem you have, is the cause of the obstruction—that it really is *their* foot on *your* hose that is causing your pain and discomfort.

Your energy, however, is yours. No one else, and no outside circumstance, has the power to constrict the flow of who you are. The way your life energy flows through your body-mind system is unique to you. When you change your focus from the other person or event and resonate with the higher purpose of your experience, you are able to restore the full flow of your life energy. In other words, you can take your own foot off your own hose. The situation may remain the same; the other person may remain the same; but you are not the same because you have restored an inner point of control over how you direct your energy, your thoughts and your actions.

During the Vietnam War, Captain Gerald Coffee, a Navy pilot, spent seven years in Vietcong concentration camps, often in solitary confinement. He survived this horrendous experience by focusing within himself. He wrote, "Without the normal distractions of everyday life, [my confinement] provided the opportunity to know myself and God far better than ever before." The external situation remained the same, but internally Captain Coffee was different. There was no one standing on the hose of his vital life energy. He returned home, not traumatized by his experience but a wise and empowered man.

This kind of story, where people have thrived and grown in the midst of major stress and dire situations, can be seen in the lives of many individuals in history—like Anne Frank, Victor Frankl, Ernest Shackleton and Nelson Mandela. They are inspirational figures for us because, like mythical heroes, they maintain their energetic focus regardless of the obstacles they encounter.

## Experiencing your energy

You can feel when your energy is flowing. When you act in ways that create order for yourself and others, notice how energized you feel. Tasks are completed with little effort. Your words match your actions. When your energy is moving in a balanced way, you always feel more positive, awake and aware.

When you act in ways that are not right for you, notice how de-energized you feel. You may get reactive in response to someone else's upset; you may not be able to decide what action would be best for you to take; you may feel confused or easily irritated. When the flow of your life energy is reduced, you automatically experience physical, emotional or mental discomfort and upset in your life.

You can pay attention to your energy in a simple way right now. Notice how you are sitting. If you are slouching, or your legs and arms are crossed, you are in a de-energizing posture that depletes your energy: you are standing on the hose of your vital force.

If you bring your spine into straighter alignment, hold your chin parallel to the ground, uncross your arms and place your feet on the floor, you are in an energizing posture. You may feel an immediate change. Are you breathing more deeply? Do you feel more relaxed, hopeful or confident? What else do you notice?

A balanced posture energizes both you and others around you. When people see you standing tall, balanced and relaxed, they respond to you positively. This is true even when you are speaking to them on the telephone. This is one of the benefits of yoga and chiropractic work—both focus on your spine to encourage an unimpeded flow of life energy. You inevitably feel better. When your spine is aligned and relaxed, it is easier to be attuned to the frequencies of what some physicists refer to as the unified field— the ocean of energy within yourself and all around you.

## Seeking answers

It is an age-old concept that energy creates life and sustains the whole creation, as described in every major religion and spiritual tradition since the dawn of humanity. The highest frequencies of this energy are known by different names: the Tao in China, the Shabd or Nam in India, the Logos in ancient Greece, the Kalima or Ism al-A'zam in the Sufi tradition, the Holy Spirit, Word or Name in the Judaeo-Christian tradition, and the Great Spirit in the Native American traditions.

Ancient cultures also recognize that this highly vibrating frequency of energy or Consciousness—Tao, Shabd, Kalima, Logos—is lowered or stepped down to progressively slower frequencies in order to sustain life on earth and in the body-mind system. In its slowed-down form, this highly vibrating energy is known as *chi* in China, *ki* in Japan, *prana* in India and *aither* (ether) in ancient Greece.

Over the course of many centuries, sages and healers have developed various practices—such as t'ai chi, chi kung and yoga —to help maintain the balanced flow of this divine energy and so allow us to rejuvenate or recharge the body-mind system. More particularly, through meditation, contemplation and prayer, this divine energy is used for spiritual development and the expansion of consciousness.

Modern culture also gives credence to the power of this energy. For example, in the Star Wars movies Luke Skywalker learns from the ancient master, Yoda, how to attune to the "Force" and use it correctly as he develops his conscious awareness and skill as a warrior.

## Scientific support

Just in the past few decades, this energy of life has become an increasingly important topic of scientific research in the fields of physics, energy psychology and the neurosciences. In fact, the National Institute of Health in the United States has funded various research grants to study energetic forms of health and healing.

James Oschman, in his book *Energy Medicine*, writes that Einstein spent his last years searching for what he called "something deeply hidden" underlying all the forms of energy recognized in physics: electricity, magnetism, heat, light, kinetic energy, sound, gravity, vibration—all the forces that fuel our physical world.

Einstein knew that every cell in the body generates an electromagnetic field, and that energy is a common denominator in the functioning of every aspect of the human body. Einstein and other physicists sensed, however, that there is a universal energetic underpinning, something bigger that serves as an organizing causal agent.

The results of their findings are documented in Lynn McTaggart's book, *The Field: The Quest for the Secret Force of the Universe*. She summarizes recent discoveries by writing that we live in "one vast quantum field," an energetic living matrix in which "we are constantly exchanging information"—with each other, with the field, and throughout the field. This, she believes, is why ancient healing traditions were and are so effective: healers access the energetic living matrix to help people balance their electromagnetic field.

There is a great deal of good science behind the concept of the energy of life; its existence is now well authenticated. Why is it not more universally known and accepted? Possibly because, while spiritual traditions long ago named and understood its various functions, modern science has not found a single unifying theory to explain life energy in a simple way so people can readily grasp and apply it in their everyday lives.

## Life energy

Understanding the concept of life energy is easier to grasp if we begin with this simple equation: Everything is energy; energy is everything.

Energy, known in Eastern traditions as *primal sound* and *light,* imbues us with life. It fills the empty spaces in our cells. It radiates an aura or energy field from and around all things: 2-year-old infants, 200-year-old trees and 20,000-year-old boulders. Your life energy isn't an abstract concept, divorced from your physical body. It infuses and gives life to your body, your feelings and your mind.

As a species we have survived for millions of years because, like all living systems, we have an innate or natural biofeedback system that allows us to adapt to our changing environment. This biofeedback system constantly monitors the state of our energy in order to maintain the balance, or homeostasis, on which our health depends. Without this internal monitor we wouldn't survive. The different systems in our body—respiratory (breathing), cardiovascular (blood flow), nervous (sensing and responding), and others—would not work to regulate the thousands of per second biochemical cellular responses that make life possible, if it were not for our ability to maintain the balanced flow of our primal life energy.

Your body-mind system is designed so that your life energy can flow in a consistently harmonious way—your biofeedback monitor sends you signals all the time about your state of harmony. Whether you feel on top of the world or sick to your stomach, your monitor is giving you signals about the way your energy is flowing in response to your perceptions about yourself, others and your environment. If you know how to pay attention, you pick up constant signals from your biofeedback monitor, telling you when your energy is flowing harmoniously and when it is stuck; when you are on track and when you are off track.

## Energy flows

Ancient cultures and various spiritual traditions have developed systems to help us understand, work with and optimize life energy and make the best use of our natural biofeedback monitors.

In the ancient healing system of Ayurveda, it is known that life energy is stepped down from ultra-high frequencies via seven major energy reservoirs in the body-mind system, known in India as chakras or spinning wheels of energy. Through these reservoirs, the stepped-down energy manifests as your ability to think and feel; it forms your physical body, governs every function and sustains every organ. It flows through multitudes of energy channels.

Twelve major channels are known in China as the Meridians, or the Twelve Officials. Their function in Chinese medicine is to maintain physical health and emotional and mental harmony, to promote long life and social well-being.

In various parts of Africa, healers attune to a vibrational blueprint of energy flows and trace these flows with their fingers to bring about balance and healing of the physical body.

In every tradition, life energy is considered self-regulating. It is meant to maintain or regain its harmonious flow so that life supports life within the vibrating, radiant, unified field.


## Energy healing

The exciting contribution of the Key of Energy is the understanding that any problem—whether pain, depression, upset, addictions, poor grades or declining sales—is a signal from your internal monitor that your life energy has come up against a roadblock of your own making. (Remember, it is your own foot on your own hose.) Your energy can be encouraged to move freely again, first by identifying the unconscious cause of the block and then by supporting your natural self-regulating tendencies that re-establish body-mind harmony.

The self-regulating process of harmonizing energy flow, as James Oschman reinforces in *Energy Medicine,* is the foundation of all ancient energy-based healing traditions. Because of the effectiveness of harmonizing energy flow, the range of Western healthcare systems that promote self-regulating methods continues to grow. Physicians are also beginning to combine allopathic medicine with energy-balancing techniques to create an effective and holistic healthcare practice. These systems, known by many names, include functional medicine, integrated medicine, complementary medicine, alternative medicine, and energy psychology.

Whatever the system, there is an acceptance that balancing the flow of energy leads to positive outcomes. Regardless of whether scientists have a unifying theory to explain energy, recipients experience an inner awareness of change that is personally significant for them.

## Activities

At the end of this and the following chapters on the Nine Keys, you'll find an *Action* that is designed to give you a practical experience of an aspect of the Key. Read through the Action first, and then, when and if you have time, focus on the activity described and slowly follow the steps as indicated. With each Action, you'll gain an understanding of how to balance your energy and create something new in your life.

# ENERGY IN ACTION

While scientists may not understand the primal energy that sustains life, the following simple chi kung practice demonstrates that your energy is palpable. You can balance your energy in many ways; one of these is through the familiar exercise that follows.

1.  Rub the palms of your hands quickly together until you notice a warm, tingling feeling from stimulating the energy in your palms and fingers. Now hold your hands facing each other about twelve inches apart. When you gently and slowly move your hands toward each other, you can generally feel a subtle pressure on your palms and fingers, as though your hands are bouncing on an invisible wave or pushing against an invisible balloon of energy.

2.  Now that you have a sense of the energy in your hands, you can use it to energize yourself. Rub your hands together again and then place them about six inches away from your belly, facing your belly button, with your fingers pointing toward each other but not quite touching. Straighten your spine and breathe slowly and deeply.

    Make sure you round out your arms so you're holding them away from your sides. Sitting or standing, point your feet directly forward or slightly in. If you are standing, flex your knees slightly. With your shoulders relaxed, continue breathing deeply. The enhanced energy flowing from your palms stimulates your body's center of vitality located below your navel.

After a few moments you may feel a shiver of energy running down your body or you may take a deep sighing breath, feel heat or coolness, or a sense of relaxation, calmness and peace. All these are signs that your energy is balancing and invigorating your system.

3. When you feel complete, slowly bring your hands to your sides. Yawn, stretch and move your body in any way you like. This circulates the energy you have just activated to all parts of your body. Then stand or sit with your eyes closed and notice how you feel.

In this simple way you can balance your life energy at any time during your day: when you feel tired, when you need an extra boost of confidence, when you are unwell or in pain, before an exam, when you feel under pressure at the office, or any time you want to feel more energized.

## HIGHLIGHTS

▲ Everything is energy. Energy is everything.

▲ Your energy is yours.

▲ The energy of life—known to all ancient cultures—is the hidden organizer or energetic matrix of modern science.

▲ You have an innate biofeedback system that constantly monitors and communicates to you the state of your energy flow.

▲ You can feel your energy and learn to keep it moving in a natural, balanced flow for your own well-being and for the benefit of all those around you.

~~~

~~~

# RESONANCE

~~~

*Everything radiates a frequency*

*and has the capacity to set a similar frequency vibrating.*

*This is called resonance.*

*It is a principle that underlies all energy healing systems*

*and all relationship interchanges.*

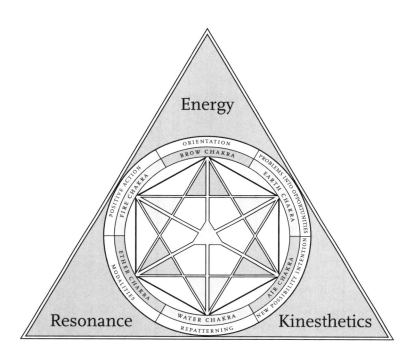

Energy

Resonance

Kinesthetics

ORIENTATION
BROW CHAKRA
PROBLEMS INTO OPPORTUNITIES
EARTH CHAKRA
POSITIVE ACTION
FIRE CHAKRA
NEW POSSIBILITY INTENTION
AIR CHAKRA
ETHER CHAKRA
MODALITIES
WATER CHAKRA
REPATTERNING

ENERGY
**RESONANCE**
KINESTHETICS
ORIENTATION
PROBLEMS
INTENTIONS
REPATTERNING
MODALITIES
ACTION

# KEY 2

~~~

*Change your resonance, change your life.*

My mother was a gifted musician and teacher, a child-prodigy who was blessed with perfect pitch, the capacity to improvise and an instinctive sense of rhythm. I learned what it was to be musical from her, and through her I had my earliest experience of resonance. Standing by the piano, I watched the felt hammers strike the wires whose vibrations miraculously produced the music of Chopin, Debussy and Bach.

Lying in bed at night as a child, listening to my mother play, I could feel the effect of the resounding notes throughout my body. Something in the music and her playing set my field vibrating with an inexplicable sense of peace. The resonance my mother created caused an energy exchange that opened me to the inner music of life and a profound sense of joy.

When I began teaching the Resonance Repatterning system in the early nineties, people were not familiar with the word "resonance." Today resonance is becoming an everyday concept. Even on the news, you hear comments about resonating with economic growth—meaning literally that we are receptive to the vibrating frequencies of economic growth. And the idea of resonance is taking on new shades of meaning as its use expands.

You may resonate with a person, which means that you like them. You may resonate with a popular singer, so you buy their CDs and attend every one of their concerts. You may resonate with a cause, which inspires you to give your active support and donate money. Your resonance means your frequencies are set vibrating by their frequencies. As a result you experience an energy exchange with that person or that cause—just as I did with my mother when she played the piano and filled our home with the harmonious sounds of music.

## Resonance and frequencies

Resonance is a natural phenomenon common to everything in the creation and it affects every detail of the quality of life you experience. You exist in fields of resonance as though in a universal piano field where all the notes of creation are played. When attuned to harmonious notes, you vibrate to joy, health, love, and the achievement of your highest potential. When blocked from this harmonious resonance, you may vibrate to depression, sickness, conflict, and an inability to manifest your potential.

Later on in this book, you'll find there are many factors, mostly unconscious, that stop you from vibrating in response to life-giving frequencies. Resonance Repatterning, as its name implies, gives you the ability to identify and transform the disharmonious frequencies you resonate with—and therefore improve your experience of life.

The following five aspects of resonance may help you understand how resonance continually operates in your life:

## 1. Frequencies

What you resonate with, or are set vibrating by, are frequencies or pulsations. These pulsations, just like your pulse and heart-beat, are measured in cycles per second. The note of C pulses at 261.63 cycles per second. Colors pulse at the equivalent of trillions of cycles per second. Every thought has a rate of pulsation, a frequency; every feeling has a frequency; every organ and cell has its own unique frequency.

If someone cuts in front of you on the freeway out of anger, their anger has a particular frequency. If you resonate with the frequencies of anger, you will probably react with feeling upset, irritated or angry. If you resonate with the frequencies of love, you are more likely to respond with understanding, humor, a blessing for the driver who is having a difficult day, or appreciation that no accident happened. Resonance determines every response you have.

## 2. Exchange

Resonance creates an energy exchange between one thing and another. When you strike the tine of a tuning fork, the other tine through resonance is set vibrating. The energy then vibrates back and forth between the two tines. When the tuning fork is vibrating, it sets other tuning forks of the same note vibrating, even across a distance, as energy is exchanged between them.

Similarly, a baby may set its parents vibrating with joy, and then the parents' joy and love in return energizes the baby even more. They set one another vibrating and exchange the energy of love back and forth, like the vibrating tines of a tuning fork.

As infants, we survived by resonating with the frequencies

of our parents, by entraining or synchronizing our energy pulsations with their vibrational patterns. Our present energy exchanges, whether coherent or non-coherent, are based on the patterns of exchange set up in infancy and early childhood. We still carry that early resonance imprint. Fortunately we have the means to identify the energy exchange patterns from our childhood and, if negative, we have the means to transform them into new and positive resonance patterns.

### 3. Attraction

The frequencies you resonate with create your own magnetic field of attraction. Your frequencies, vibrating back and forth in an energy exchange within your own body-mind system, create a magnetic field which attracts similar frequencies. This means that if you want to change an experience, you need to change the resonance within yourself that attracts what you experience.

What you resonate with impacts your thoughts and feelings; resonance decides the state of your physical health and your ability to succeed. The more you resonate with life-supporting goals, aspirations and priorities, the greater the magnetic field of attraction that makes the active achievement of your priorities possible.

### 4. Power

You have the power to change your resonance. You have the choice to consciously change the chaotic frequencies of anger and fear to the coherent frequencies of love, confidence and hope. When your field is unconsciously pulsing with the frequencies of anger or frustration, for example, you will attract this kind of frequency from others. You may wonder why someone reacts to you with anger or sternness. Like tuning forks, both of you are vibrating in an energy exchange. It may look like the other person is the problem, but you too are involved in the vibrating exchange.

Any problem you have involves a two-way resonance—the other person's and your own. When your field is pulsing with the coherent frequencies of love and appreciation, you will find yourself attracting people and events in which these loving frequencies are amplified and enjoyed.

## 5. Entrainment or synchronization

Resonance creates change through the principle of entrainment, by which one frequency brings another into synchronization. When you read in the paper about a potentially violent situation in which one person remains calm and a crime is averted, you are reading about resonance and synchronization in action: the chaotic frequencies of the perpetrator are soothed by synchronizing with the calm frequencies of the other person.

The more coherent your frequencies are, the more you create coherence in others. This is why people will sometimes tell you they feel better just from talking with you. As I entrained with my mother's love of music and the beauty of her playing, so others may entrain with your coherence.

## Research on resonance

Imagine you are sitting alone in a softly lit room. There is someone you don't know in the next room. Both of you are wired to an EEG machine that reads your brainwaves.

You are asked to relax, settle into the silence and become aware of your connection with the other person. As you breathe deeply, your brainwave patterns become more and more coherent; the right and left sides of your brain become synchronized; your bandwidth expands and you attune to a wider range of frequencies in the field.

The researchers watch as the brainwave patterns of the other person begin to synchronize with yours. You and the person in the next room establish what Lynn McTaggart describes as a coherent domain. As a result, even if the other person is disturbed by a sudden noise that disrupts his or her brainwave patterns, they will quickly come back into alignment with the synchronized patterns of the coherent domain you have jointly established. It's not just that both brainwave patterns regain a state of common order; they actually regain the same frequency patterns in the same parts of the brain.

We are resonant beings who exist in a field of frequencies shared by everyone. We influence all others, for better or for worse. We are influenced by others according to the frequencies in them that we resonate with. The more coherent the frequencies we emit, the more we nudge other resonant beings toward a higher degree of order and well-being, and the less we are affected by the non-coherent de-energizing frequencies of others.

## Decoding resonance

In your everyday life, resonance probably isn't the first thing on your mind. It is important to realize, however, that resonance plays out in your life down to the smallest detail. A common situation is resonance with an unconscious fear of not being good enough. This resonance is like wearing dark glasses stamped with the words *not good enough*. Everywhere you look, you see *not good enough*. The direct result of your resonance with this fear is that you may find yourself being critical and judgmental of yourself or of everything out there—whether the organization you work for, other people, the government or the state of the world. Nothing is good enough!

If you identify with these *not good enough* glasses, you will tend to attract situations that resonate with "not good enough": people who let you down, exclude you or hurt you; relationships that don't nurture you; jobs that are below your skill level and don't pay you what you need; events that bring failure, disappointment, stress and upset.

If you recognize yourself in any of these situations, imagine now the glasses you would rather wear. You can choose to resonate with the frequencies of confidence and high value for yourself and others—choosing new glasses that say "I am of great value to this world, as are others." When you radiate this new quality of valuing yourself, you will find value everywhere you look, in everything you do and in all the valuable people you choose to work with and relate to. Each person, through resonance, will respond to the more harmonious notes you're now playing.

## Global change

The power of resonance also applies in businesses, organizations and countries; with bosses and employees, leaders and teams, governments and populations of all kinds.

If a business wants you as their customer, they need to set you vibrating to their resonant frequency. If you, as a boss, want your employees to achieve certain goals, then you need to resonate with a motivating vision, and your employees also need to resonate with your vision and the goals that in turn support their own personal growth and the achievement of their potential.

In any successful business or organization, there is a resonant energy exchange between the employees, the work itself, the company's vision and the customers. In every country, there is a resonant energy exchange between the people, their leaders, the country's laws and its cultural behaviors.

World philosophies have an especially powerful resonance. Great beings throughout time, devoted to a life of divine purpose, developed highly refined and conscious frequencies that continue to set us vibrating through their teachings. When you resonate with their words, you attract and live their qualities of unconditional love. When, through spiritual practice, you move into resonance with the frequency of their truth, you are drawn closer to realizing the divine potential they demonstrated.

## Quality of resonance

Positive quantum change begins with the power of one. The more you change your resonance and become aligned with the open flow of unconditional love, the more you will express this resonance in all your words and actions.

Resonance is more than an inspirational idea. The phrase "Change your resonance, change your life" is quite literally true. Because you are interconnected through resonance with all other beings, the uplifting personal changes you make immediately radiate through the unified field and, through resonance, make the frequencies of uplifting change available to all who are attuned to these frequencies.

# RESONANCE IN ACTION

A powerful way to examine resonance is to use your voice—a sound that vibrates through every cell in your body and to those around you. In this exercise, you'll use your voice to feel and move from a chaotic resonance to a well-ordered resonance.

First, imagine what the sound of depression might be. It could be a very low note, a moaning or sighing sound. Make whatever sound feels appropriate and expresses your resonance with depression. Notice how you feel as this sound vibrates through your body and what posture your body automatically takes as a result of this sound.

Now make a sound that expresses your resonance with anger, which is more energizing than depression but still chaotic. Notice how this sound vibrates in your body, changes your facial expression and your posture.

Now imagine and make the sound that expresses your resonance with confidence. What sound does confidence make as expressed through your voice? How does your body respond as it resonates with this new frequency? Notice what happens to your eyes and your facial expression. You may feel more energized as the sound of confidence plays through your body-mind energy field.

Finally, imagine and make a sound that expresses the open and flowing responsiveness of unconditional love. Notice how your body posture responds to the resonance of this sound. How do you feel as you resonate with the sound of unconditional love?

Unconditional love is the universal frequency of life
—and who you are at your core. The more you resonate
with love, the more you will experience love in your life,
and the more you will be able to give love to others.

# HIGHLIGHTS

▲ You can change the effect of your past and your hopes for
the future by changing your resonance in the present.

▲ Because you exist in a field of energy, what you resonate with
in this field of frequencies determines what you experience.

▲ You emit a frequency of light and sound energy that attracts
other people through resonance.

▲ Disharmonious (non-coherent) frequencies you resonate
with have the power to set others vibrating, but only if they
too resonate with these frequencies, and vice versa.

▲ Harmonious (coherent) frequencies you resonate with have
the power to entrain and modify disharmonious (non-
coherent) frequencies in yourself and others.

▲ This is how personal quantum change leads to global quantum change.

~~~

# THE KINESTHETIC SENSE

~~~

*The kinesthetic sense is our innate body-mind knowing*

*of what frequencies are coherent and life-enhancing,*

*and what frequencies are not.*

*Desires, psychological patterns and energy imbalances*

*cause us to override our kinesthetic sense.*

*The Resonance Repatterning system*

*and Resonance Kinesiology*

*enable us to restore our awareness*

*of our kinesthetic sense.*

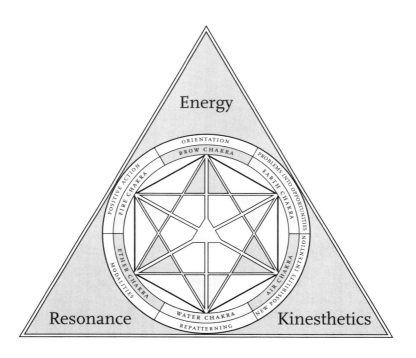

ENERGY
RESONANCE
KINESTHETICS
ORIENTATION
PROBLEMS
INTENTIONS
REPATTERNING
MODALITIES
ACTION

# KEY 3

~~~

*You are wired for coherence and self-healing.*

A friend was sitting in an outdoor restaurant when a blue-eyed husky came up to her with obvious interest. The owner was a lady at the table next to hers; soon they were both talking about the beauty of the husky, who was wearing an "in service" halter. The owner shared that she had epileptic seizures; her dog, like all animals, she said, was highly attuned to electrical frequencies. He was trained to recognize the changing electrical impulses that began ten minutes before her seizures actually started and he would signal her to lie down in a safe place, so that, caught unawares, she wouldn't fall and harm herself.

Most animal lovers have fascinating stories about the kind of inner knowing and sensitivity animals exhibit. Children too. You may remember as a child how you knew certain things: whether you trusted and felt safe with someone, or did not. This is your kinesthetic sense at work—your natural inborn sense of knowing. In the same way that most of us are born with the sense of seeing, hearing, smelling and tasting, so most of us are also born with the kinesthetic sense, which includes touch, movement and gut responses.

In times past we were dependent on our kinesthetic sense

for our survival: attuned to the frequencies of plants, we knew if they were medicinal or poisonous; we knew whether a potentially dangerous animal would attack or pass by without harming us; whether an earthquake was about to happen; whether the changing seasons would bring storms or floods. There was an exchange of energy between people and nature that appears uncanny to the majority of us, who have lost our connection to this inner knowing of energy frequencies.

Once I sat on a flat rooftop on a Hopi reservation watching the rain dancers in the street below, in ceremonial dress, disguised behind their masks, rhythmically dance in the desert heat of a cloudless Arizona day. The Hopi people needed just a small amount of rain for the survival of their corn. I couldn't connect with the idea that dancing might create rain; but in the late afternoon, driving back to where I was staying, I suddenly noticed clouds forming in the azure sky over the village land. The rain poured down for ten minutes and then the clouds were gone. The Hopi's kinesthetic sense tells them how and when to connect with the natural, coherent frequencies they need. Year after year they dance, call on the rain, and survive.

## Your felt sense

Each of your senses, like a satellite dish, picks up frequencies: the eyes pick up the frequencies of light; the ears, the frequencies of sound and rhythm; the tongue, the frequencies of taste; the nose, the frequencies of smell. Your kinesthetic sense, your inner knowing, picks up the frequencies of your own thoughts and emotional responses, as well as the frequencies in your environment—just like the husky did.

Regardless of which sense is engaged, frequencies from all the senses are transmitted to your brain as electrical impulses.

Your brain decodes these frequencies so you see forms, colors and textures; hear sounds, music and words; taste food and smell fragrances. When the brain decodes the frequencies picked up by your kinesthetic sense, a cascade of chemical neurotransmitters floods your body and creates body responses and feelings: you feel good, you feel bad; you feel tension in your gut or you feel relaxed; your breathing becomes shallow or slow and deep; your heartbeat speeds up or slows down; you feel angry or happy.

Awareness of your body responses and feelings is known as your "felt sense." Directly connected to your autonomic nervous system and your neurotransmitter cascades, your felt sense lets you know in any situation whether you feel comfortable or not.

## A lost sense

When we were children, our felt sense, like an animal's, was highly developed. Unfortunately it was generally ignored at best and belittled at worst in the adult world we inhabited. Shamed out of honestly responding to what we felt, we became confused. What we absolutely knew as our truth from within ourselves was often polarized by what adults told us was true. Who to trust—ourselves or them?

In response to this confusion, most of us, as children, abdicated the throne of our inner knowing and learned to ignore our body signals. Out of trust for the adults in our world, or dependence on them for love, we stopped accessing our truth and telling our truth. The price we paid was a loss of trust in our body responses and a loss of confidence in our power to know what is right or not right for us.

We moved into the discomforting feeling of "I am wrong, others are right," or simply into a state of hopelessness that we would ever be understood. Unable to express the truth of our felt sense, we stopped tuning in to the frequencies, both within ourselves and without, that tell us how to live well and safely.

## Available 24/7

Fortunately, the kinesthetic sense—your body-mind knowing of energy frequencies—is always with you, even if ignored. It operates at unconscious levels 24/7 whether you are aware of it or not. Your kinesthetic sense is inseparably linked to your somatic nervous system, which picks up what is going on within yourself and in your environment and, through electrical signals, fires your muscles in response.

It is also linked to your autonomic nervous system, which takes care of 90% of the unconscious functions that make life possible. Your autonomic nervous system insures that your food is digesting while you read these pages, and that your brain has enough oxygen to understand each phrase. It manages complex interactions simultaneously in trillions of cells while you simply turn this page.

If you've ever come across the artwork of Alex Grey, you've seen illustrations of the body from the inside: the delicate network of nerves that branch their way to every millimeter of skin and link to the intricate geometry of the energy field beyond. Through your kinesthetic sense, you are a highly developed sensing device, reaching out to access every single pulsing event within yourself, in your environment and in the infinite field beyond. The question is: How can you easily and efficiently access the helpful range of frequency information that your kinesthetic sense picks up? The answer to this question opens up a new world of information; it is what makes breakthrough quantum change possible.

## An ocean of frequencies

A friend once described to me an experience she had with her first scuba dive in the tropics: "Amazing," she wrote, "after the bubbles cleared I looked around and realized I'd entered a whole new kingdom. It was complete, fully functioning and utterly beautiful. Most of us don't even know it's there. I'm changed forever by finding this ancient world that lives so silently beneath the skin of the ocean!"

I felt this way when I came across the field of applied kinesiology and had my first experience of what I call muscle checking. The subtle information my conscious adult mind knew little of suddenly became available. A whole new world opened up for me. I had found the key to something that had always been present: my kinesthetic sense.

Through the tool of muscle checking, I now had access to the beautiful and ordered world of frequencies and resonance that were my natural heritage. Muscle checking—the simple application of pressure on a muscle and observing its response—was the connecting link between the invisible frequencies I was immersed in, my autonomic nervous system, and my innate capacity to self-heal.

## Pieces of the puzzle

Physicians, osteopaths and physical therapists have long understood the importance of the movement of energy or electrical impulses through muscles. The kinesiology they used was a technique that involved putting pressure on a muscle and observing its on/off, strong/relaxed response to determine which muscles were receiving nerve impulses. When a particular muscle remained strong under pressure, the practitioner knew that nerve impulses were flowing to that muscle; if the muscle weakened under pressure, it indicated a lack of nerve impulse to that muscle.

Another piece of the puzzle fell into place with the brilliant evolution of Applied Kinesiology, also known as muscle testing. A chiropractor named Dr. John Thie realized that the application of pressure on a muscle, while observing its on/off, strong/relaxed response, could be used to indicate which of the twelve acupuncture meridians were receiving energy—too much or too little.

Now muscle testing had a new and expanded theory: the muscle response (physical) could be reliably used to access information about electromagnetic energy flows through the meridians (non-physical). The results were there to be seen. Good results: the Touch for Health method developed by Dr. Thie rapidly became a viable and popular system of complementary healthcare.

Of great significance to me, Applied Kinesiology or muscle testing opened the possibility for using this tool to verify not just electrical nerve impulses to muscles and energy balance in the meridian system, but also, I realized, invisible energy flows in the whole body-mind field.

A further evolution came in the late 1980s when many people in the self-help field began to experiment with muscle testing. Moving beyond the meridians, practitioners used the on/off muscle response to provide information about unconscious perceptions, about hidden belief systems and about the forgotten earlier experiences underlying a particular problem.

At this point in my career as a healthcare practitioner, I used the on/off response of my finger muscles to ascertain which modality a client needed. I had not yet made the connection that our kinesthetic sense naturally mediates not just physical nerve impulses and meridian energies, but other frequencies as well.

## The body knows

A breakthrough moment came in the late 1970s when I was working on an eight-year-old child I'll call Tommy, who had cerebral palsy. Since birth, his legs had been crossed over each other and his elbows bent and locked to his rib cage. His fists were tightly closed and he couldn't speak. Each week his mother would carry him in and place him on my massage table. I would do Polarity Therapy and Cross Fiber Therapy on him, in an attempt to release the intensity of his muscular contractions.

One day, with his mother's permission, I decided to experiment with muscle checking. Could I use the on/off muscle response of my own fingers to learn more about what his body-mind needed? I began to question exactly what he might need, using the on/off, strong/relaxed response of my finger muscles to let me know *Yes, this supports Tommy's system* or *No, this does not support Tommy's system.* Muscle checking indicated that he needed a particular Polarity contact—cupping my fingers in front and behind his ears and slowly rotating both his ears for ten minutes. I knew, theoretically, that this was a wonderfully relaxing Polarity contact, but generally a practitioner holds the contact for about a minute. Ten minutes was a long time!

Breathing slowly and deeply I began the rotation. Tommy's mother and I watched in silence. After about five minutes we could see his body relaxing. And then slowly it happened: his arms began to open. Bit by bit, over the final five minutes of the ear rotation his arms opened until they were lying almost flat on the table.

Tommy's arms returned to their tightly bent position as soon as the session was over, but Tommy, his mother and I now had a felt sense of what was possible. Equally thrilling, it was clear that Tommy's body-mind frequency field knew what modality he needed in that moment for his arms to open. Similar sessions followed, all with differing modalities. Gradually his arms began to stay open until, some months later, Tommy was able for the first time in his life to hold a spoon and feed himself.

This was the power of the kinesthetic sense accessed through muscle checking. Tommy's system always knew exactly what he needed. Because we are all parts of the universal hologram, indivisibly connected and unified, I was able to use kinesiology—my own on/off muscle response—as a tool to pick up the electrical messages from his autonomic nervous system and verify which modality he needed for his self-healing.

Now I knew there was a natural connection between the body's nervous system, the subtle energies it responded to, and the muscles it fired. What's more, I could use kinesiology to access that response, that inborn sense, in support of another person's self-healing.

## The next question

But there still remained the question of why people are controlled by behaviors they do not want. Eventually I realized the answer had everything to do with earlier experiences when we shut down our awareness of our kinesthetic sense, that inner knowing of what is coherent, right and true for us.

Experiences of neglect and abuse when our life needs were

not met caused us to move into resonance with survival patterns and compensating behaviors. It is our resonance with these non-coherent frequency patterns that overrides our awareness of our kinesthetic sense.

Our body-mind stores the frequencies of everything that's ever happened to us: our thoughts, feelings, beliefs, memories, compensating attitudes and behaviors. Our memory database is like our computer's hard drive. The past frequencies imprinted on this hard drive directly affect how we operate in the present.

Our body-mind constantly receives, monitors and measures new inputs of frequency information. The new information—our present experiences—and the past, unconscious information in our database have instant communication channels.

If a new frequency—an idea, a comment, an action—even partially resonates with the unconscious information stored in our database, we will inevitably default to the neural pathways and memory imprints of the old information: our automatic responses take over and drive our words and actions, regardless of our desire to handle a present situation differently.

This is why we can be hijacked by our feelings—anger, fear, sadness, overwhelm—before we are even aware of a thought or event that may have triggered them. The old stories we resonate with in our database take control and we find ourselves overriding our kinesthetic sense, which knows the appropriate response in the present moment.

## Evolution of muscle checking

For some time, I used the on/off muscle response to determine the energizing or de-energizing effects of modalities, actions, words, foods and anything else that occurred to me. Early on, for instance, I discovered that the word *testing* weakens muscles, and I therefore changed the name of what I was doing from muscle "testing" to muscle "checking," which proved to be more energizing for my clients.

Gradually I made the connection that muscle checking could be used to access information about nerve impulses and all subtle energy flows (not just meridian flows). Thanks to clients like Tommy, I discovered that I could muscle check on myself to find out what another person's frequency field needed to create more harmony and balance in their life or body.

My understanding that all the information in our body-mind database is stored as frequencies led to the next step. If disharmony in the body-mind comes from a lack of resonance with life-supporting frequencies, then why not use muscle checking to locate this lack of resonance and to discover the modality that will correct the disharmony?

Through experiment in my clinical practice, I formulated a new system of muscle checking and self-healing based entirely on frequencies, resonance and coherence. The system includes both a *resonance* muscle check to locate the source of the disharmony we resonate with and therefore experience, and a *coherence* muscle check to determine what will change our negative resonance and re-establish harmony. This new form of applied kinesiology, which I now call Resonance Kinesiology, is an integral part of the self-healing system, Resonance Repatterning.

## Resonance muscle checking

Resonance muscle checking is important because it is the frequencies you resonate with that manifest as your experiences and attitudes in life. To change your experience and attitudes, you need to know which frequencies you resonate with, and which ones you need to resonate with but don't.

Through resonance muscle checking I discovered that even outwardly successful, vivacious people were often resonating with "I'm not good enough," "I'm ugly," or "I'm not attractive." They actually muscle checked "on" for these de-energizing beliefs — and resonated with their outcomes too: an unfulfilling job, a dysfunctional relationship, a sense of isolation or lack of self-confidence regardless of their success.

Once we become aware of our resonance with such life-depleting frequencies, we can transform this limiting resonance. Resonance muscle checking indicates the life-enhancing frequencies we need (but do not resonate with) in order to activate our natural resonance with good health, happiness and fulfilling relationships.

*Resonance muscle checking* is a tool that helps you find the unconscious frequencies your body-mind system needs to neutralize, and the unconscious frequencies your system needs to strengthen and amplify. This is how you discover what old glasses you are wearing and what new ones you are ready to put on.

*Coherence muscle checking* is a tool that helps you find the modalities you need, like Tommy's Polarity contacts, to neutralize your de-energizing resonance and strengthen your energizing resonance. Changing your resonance in this way is how you can change your experience of life.

## Coherence muscle checking

The coherence muscle check proves that nothing in the creation is neutral. Every frequency either energizes you or does not; it either brings more coherence to your system or it does not. The on/off response of the coherence muscle check lets you know whether your frequencies are amplified or diminished in response to another frequency—in the form of a statement, question, or what is called a cue.

This means that you can use the coherence on/off muscle check, with training, to make self-empowering choices about what energizes you and what creates more coherence, order and balance in your life—and, with their permission, in the lives of others too.

The on/off muscle check is simply a physiological response to messages from the autonomic nervous system. Since the kinesthetic sense and the autonomic nervous system are designed to pick up frequencies from anyone and anything in this holographic universe, I was able—just as the husky did, picking up its owner's frequencies—to use my muscle check as a tool for picking up Tommy's frequencies.

Through my questioning (cues) and using my own fingers for muscle checking, I was able to use the on/off response to find out the frequency Tommy's system was emitting: what modality his system was saying Yes to, for his greater coherence and self-healing, and for how long he needed it.

The effectiveness of coherence muscle checking depends on the number of statements or options available to you. The autonomic nervous system simply responds to cues; it is not a truth check, but a relative response, limited by the range of whatever you put before it. If you make just one option available, then the muscle response, with no room for comparison, may be "on" for something that creates an improved sense of well-being even though many other options might be better for you. On the other hand, if you make five options available, the muscle response may now be "off" for the first option and "on" for the second or the fourth—because your frequencies indicate that those modalities will serve you better than the first option.

In my session with Tommy, I had hundreds of options in my database. Rotating his ears for ten minutes would never have come up as an option if I hadn't had it available in my mental database. Coherence muscle checking is only as good as the options you provide. It never gives an absolute "truth." Everything in coherence muscle checking is relative, depending on your (or the practitioner's) knowledge of the most coherent options available.

The coherence muscle check can also vary according to what you unconsciously resonate with. Without understanding resonance, it is easy to misuse the coherence muscle check as a truth check. For example, if you muscle check "I have cancer" and you get an "on" response, this does not indicate what is true. It may simply be that you resonate with the word "cancer."

A new student of mine who had learned the coherence muscle check was going to use it to decide whether he should accept job A or job B. What he did not realize, I told him, was that if he had an unconscious resonance with being overworked and underpaid, he would muscle check "on" for the job that fit this negative resonance. He would think he was muscle checking for which job was in his highest and best interest (for what would create more *coherence*) when in fact he was muscle checking his *resonance*—which might be "on" for being overworked and underpaid. With the resonance muscle check, he verified the unconscious frequency patterns he resonated with. After changing this resonance, he was easily able to decide for himself, without muscle checking, which job to take—neither A nor B!

## A basic theory

My theory about muscle checking and Resonance Kinesiology is based on the following concepts:

- Everything you have said, thought and done is stored in your database as both coherent and non-coherent frequencies.

- Your autonomic nervous system transmits information from your frequency database as electrical impulses.

- Your reflex muscle responses are controlled by your autonomic nervous system.

- All muscles respond in a binary, strong/relaxed, on/off way to the transmission of electrical impulses.

- The on/off muscle response is a physiological reflex to messages from your autonomic nervous system—and kinesiology or muscle checking is a way to observe these reflex responses.

- With *resonance muscle checking*, your muscles' binary response reveals the non-coherent frequencies you unconsciously resonate with, and the coherent frequencies you want to resonate with but unconsciously do not.

- With *coherence muscle checking*, your muscles' binary response reveals the options that re-establish coherence and order, allowing you to change your resonance with what does not support you and your life, into resonance with the frequencies that do support you and your life.

- You can access your own frequencies in a self-session by muscle checking on yourself.

- You can access the frequencies of another, with permission, when you give them a session.

## Underlying resonance

A Resonance Repatterning practitioner worked with a gifted woman I'll call Mary, who had been a partner in a design firm for nearly twenty-five years. She wanted Resonance Repatterning sessions for a particular problem: she lived in chronic fear that her business partner was going to break up their partnership.

In her first session, it became apparent that the problem was her unmanageable temper tantrums. Mary simply "went off" around her partner and customers in ways that made no sense. No matter what she did, or how often she and her partner discussed ways to cope, nothing made any difference. In spite of her temper tantrums their business was successful, but her behavior had taken its toll in terms of trust as well as on her ability to focus creatively when new opportunities appeared.

Mary's behavior was unpredictable, muscle checking showed, because an earlier experience she still resonated with was continuing to control her life in the present. Her resonance with the old story was so strong that any situation remotely similar to it reactivated her unresolved, unmet needs from the past. Her tantrums were simply the way she would have liked to respond as an infant to communicate that her need for safety, protection and an orderly environment was not being met.

The *resonance muscle check* showed that she unconsciously resonated with tantrums (an "on" muscle response) and did not resonate with safety, protection and the orderly environment she longed for (an "off" muscle response). Resonating with disorder, Mary's temper tantrums continually created more disorder. Her real problem was her own resonance.

The *coherence muscle check* indicated that to resolve this negative pattern, she needed to transform her resonance with an earlier experience—which turned out to be an abusive one. Mary

49

revealed that persistent and long-term abuse had taken many forms. Coherence muscle checking indicated it wasn't necessary to know the details of her story, only to find the emotionally-charged aspects she resonated with that continued to trigger her tantrums.

Because her world from the time of infancy was so unsafe, she had formed beliefs that nothing was safe and that change was unsafe. She resonated with the perception that life could only be managed by rigid control. This meant that when her control was threatened she went into a tantrum. Mary's need to be in control served her well when she was managing jobs for her customers, but the slightest hint of non-control set off a cascade of her old stress and survival signals.

In the first several sessions when her resonance with old stories and unmet needs was identified through muscle check-ing, Mary and the practitioner were able to transform this reso-nance from "change is unsafe," to "I am safely held and loved, no matter what." After several months of repatterning sessions, Mary was able to listen to her *felt sense*, which gave her clear signals about when she felt safe and when she didn't.

It now became safe for Mary to trust her business partner, her customers and her own honest reactions in new situations. If shades of her old behavior showed up, she and her partner would stop and ask, "What feels unsafe right now?" In this way her felt sense of safety and appropriate boundaries was honored, and her resonance with the vibratory frequency of safety was repatterned from the inside out.

## Learning to muscle check

By now you may be wondering how you can learn to muscle check for yourself. I have found that learning muscle checking through a book does not do justice to you or the technique. Too often people learn to muscle check in a few minutes, experiment with it, and after a few days discard it, claiming "it doesn't work." Also, as we've seen, muscle checking without the clarity of a structured system can be unreliable.

Since both resonance and coherence muscle checking are such essential tools in the Resonance Repatterning system, the Resonance Repatterning teachers demonstrate the theory and practice in all the beginning seminars. Everyone learns how to apply both resonance and coherence muscle checking with ease in the context of a self-session and in sessions given to others.

Resonance Repatterning students also learn to use muscle checking in increasingly refined ways: to determine the specific levels and areas of the body-mind where the frequency block is held, and the umbilical level where life-supporting frequencies have been unknowingly cancelled.

## Your felt sense

What you are learning right now is how to become aware of your kinesthetic sense—through your felt sense/body responses. By doing the activities at the end of each Key, you are beginning to access this innate resource and listen to its messages.

Your felt sense is not your intuition or a thinking process; it is your body-feeling perception of an aspect of the kinesthetic sense, just as color and sound are body-feeling perceptions of the visual and auditory senses.

You pick up on frequency information all the time; your felt sense is simply your awareness of your body-feeling responses to this frequency information. The felt sense is a physiological response that tells you how you are feeling in any situation. The more you use it, the more your felt sense becomes a conscious part of your everyday awareness, in the same way that seeing and hearing are a part of your everyday awareness.

## Listening to your felt sense

Your initial experience with your felt sense may seem overly subtle, especially if you are accustomed to relying on your brain for answers. In the activities that follow, you are introduced to an activity designed to strengthen your resonance with something you'd like to do or accomplish. You are encouraged to use your felt sense to select a modality whose frequencies match and amplify the frequencies of the task you'd like to accomplish or attract.

Read through the entire Action instructions first, and then go back to #1, breathing slowly and deeply. Take your time as you follow along, perhaps even writing down the statement you create in #2, the modality you select in #3 and any sensation or change you experience in #4. If you like, you can go back and try another modality. Note your felt sense responses each time you do.

## KINESTHETICS IN ACTION

This activity introduces you to the use of your felt sense. Follow along with the instructions and take time for each step. For most people, the feeling response that comes from the felt sense has been ignored for decades, replaced by an over-emphasis on left-brain analytical thinking. So be patient. You may be obtaining information in an unfamiliar way, so it is natural if at first it feels strange.

1. Start by breathing slowly and deeply. Feel yourself relaxing. Now bring to mind something you'd like to accomplish that has, so far, felt difficult or out of reach.

2. Say aloud: "Yes, I enhance my resonance with unconditional love today by (name the thing you'd like to accomplish) and I choose the best modality from the list below to help me resonate with my goal."

   If you are not sure what unconditional love means to you as an ideal, here is a simple definition: unconditional love refers to a flowing, harmonious response to ourselves, to others and to the Divine.

3. Scan the short list of modalities below using your felt sense to select the one that feels right to you. You reconnect with your felt sense by tuning in to how your body and feelings are responding to each one listed.

   You are looking for the one modality in relation to your goal that sends out a "feel good" response. The right modality lights you up in a subtle way because it improves your resonance with the quality of your goal. It feels like an inner switch going on; you may suddenly take a deep breath or feel your spine straightening or simply feel relaxed and grounded. This is an inner sensing exercise—you are attuning to your body-feeling feedback response, which is both immediate and subtle. Your felt sense doesn't need to be learned; it is a natural, spontaneous response. You simply need to become aware of it.

## All coherent modalities input coherent energy

*Energizing modalities* stimulate the body-mind field when stuck energy needs to be activated. *Soothing modalities* calm an over-stimulated or stressed nervous system when the relax response needs strengthening and energy flows need to come back into balance. Give yourself plenty of time to complete the action.

## Energizing modalities

- Clap your hands all around your body—to release stagnation.

- Free movement: move in whatever way your body wants—to enhance your energy flow.

- Vigorously shake out your hands, arms, legs, body and jaw—to release stress, tension and resistance.

## Soothing modalities

- Slow, deep breathing with eyes open or closed—to calm your fight-flight autonomic nervous system stress responses.

- Light a candle and look at the flame with soft eyes—or imagine that you are looking at a candle flame. Breathe slowly and deeply and feel your mind calming down.

- Walk around in a natural outdoor environment, or imagine that you are in nature—at the beach, in the mountains, in the woods, by a still lake, in a meadow of wild flowers—absorbing the gifts of peace, beauty and abundance.

4. Now use your felt sense to notice how your resonance has shifted. Perhaps you have the energy to begin what you would like to accomplish; perhaps you are free of doubt; perhaps you can see and focus more clearly on the next step you need to take. You might want to continue doing the modality for a few days and notice what happens in relation to your goal.

You are now applying the Key of Kinesthetics through your felt sense responses. You have learned to create a context and to select a modality to strengthen your resonance with something you'd like to attract or accomplish. Modalities consist of coherent energy frequencies, no matter which ones your felt sense chooses. When you use your felt sense to choose the modality that most lights you up, you can trust it is an effective and efficient way to balance your energy.

# HIGHLIGHTS

▲ The kinesthetic sense is your natural, inborn sense of knowing based on the brain interpreting the frequencies the kinesthetic sense picks up from within yourself, from your environment and from the unified field.

▲ Your autonomic nervous system responds to the frequency inputs of your kinesthetic sense by initiating neurotransmitter cascades and biochemical responses to all parts of the body.

▲ Muscle checking is your on/off muscle reflex response to information from your autonomic nervous system.

▲ Your felt sense is your awareness of your body and feeling responses to neurotransmitter cascades activated by your autonomic nervous system.

▲ The Resonance Repatterning system includes two kinds of muscle checking: the *resonance muscle check,* which identifies the frequencies you resonate with, and the *coherence muscle check,* which identifies the modalities and actions that bring you more coherence, order and self-healing.

▲ The fact that you are directly connected to your kinesthetic sense, your autonomic nervous system, your reflex muscle response and your felt sense makes it possible to learn exactly what your body-mind needs for self-healing.

▲ Your body-mind system is wired for coherence, self-healing and positive transformation.

~~~

## The Evolving Field of Kinesiology

**Kinesiology**

1. The study of muscles and movement within the body; used by physical educators, coaches and physiotherapists.

2. The on-off response to pressure on a muscle indicating the presence of nerve impulses; used by physical therapists and osteopaths.

**Applied Kinesiology**

Developed by Dr. George Goodheart in 1964 as a diagnostic and therapeutic intervention for doctors and chiropractors. He strengthened the "off response" muscle to help maintain a spinal adjustment.

**Touch for Health**

In the 1970s, Dr. John Thie, with Dr. Goodheart's blessing, created the Touch for Health system that lay people could do on each other, using muscle testing to identify the flow of energy through Chinese acupuncture meridians. This system made Applied Kinesiology known and popular around the world.

**Health Kinesiology**

Many new systems are based on kinesiology or muscle testing.

*Three-in-One Concepts* for stress and emotional pain. *Bio Kinesiology* for nutritional supplements. *Clinical Kinesiology* uses the body as a bio computer. Newer systems include *Psych-K* and *Body Talk*.

**Educational Kinesiology**

Developed by Dr. Paul and Gail Dennison, based on the brain-body connection.

*Brain Gym* uses physical movements that integrate the front-back, top-bottom and left-right brain areas and hemispheres for improved learning.

**Resonance Kinesiology**

Developed by Chloe Faith Wordsworth in the 1990s, RK determines patterns of resonance and coherence throughout the body-mind system.

*The Resonance Repatterning System/Holographic Repatterning* uses muscle checking to identify negative frequency patterns you resonate with and the positive frequency patterns you do not resonate with. Also uses self-muscle checking to select modalities (from sound, color, movement, etc.) to re-establish positive resonance for optimal well-being in any situation.

# Resonance Kinesiology

### Kinesthetics
The principle of inner knowing through the body's muscle sense of all energy frequencies, including frequencies in the unified field of which we are a part.

### The Kinesthetic Sense
The body-mind knowing through touch, movement and gut responses to thoughts, emotions and to the environment. Responses are transmitted as electrical impulses by the nervous system to the brain, body and muscular system.

### Neurotransmitter Cascades
Biochemical responses that send instant stress or relax signals throughout the body in response to an inner or outer cue (negative or positive thoughts, emotions, sounds, words, sights, smells, tastes or touch, etc.).

### Resonance Kinesiology
In the Resonance Repatterning system, this is the on/off muscle response to electrical impulses via the autonomic nervous system. The on/off muscle response tells us which frequency patterns we do and do not resonate with, and what coherent modalities will activate our natural resonance for body-mind well-being.

### Felt Sense
A body-feeling response to neurotransmitter cascades that tells us how we feel—tense, stressed, relaxed, happy, etc.

### Resonance Muscle Check
Muscle checking on self or another for the on/off muscle response to a positive or negative cue or statement, indicating unconscious resonance.

### Coherence Muscle Check
Muscle checking on self for the on/off muscle response to identify the modality needed for changing resonance and creating greater coherence and order.

### General Muscle Check
Resonance muscle check for system-wide resonance.

### Specific Muscle Check
Resonance muscle check for resonance at a specific area, level and/or age.

### Initial Muscle Responses
*On* You resonate with a negative cue. *Off* You do not resonate with a positive cue. *Umbilically On or Off* You have zero energy for the positive aspect of the cue.

~~~

# ORIENTATION TO LIFE

~~~

*When we resonate with orientation to life,*

*we naturally face the direction*

*that most nourishes us and others—*

*the direction that brings purpose to our lives.*

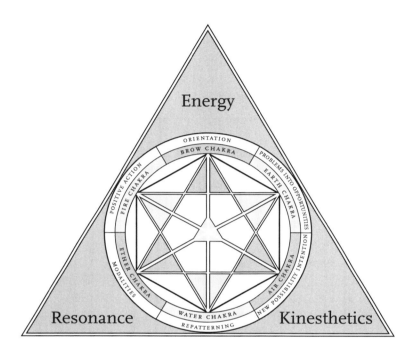

ENERGY
RESONANCE
KINESTHETICS
**ORIENTATION**
PROBLEMS
INTENTIONS
REPATTERNING
MODALITIES
ACTION

# KEY 4

~~~~

*Oriented, you face the direction*

*that nurtures your soul.*

You can witness the power of orientation when you watch a baby in its first moments of life. If the prenatal experience was harmonious and nurturing, and the birth process free of trauma, the newborn, when placed on the mother's belly, will move *by itself* toward the mother's breast. The baby has an inborn sense of orientation to life that allows it to naturally connect with its new source of nourishment in the outside world and to reconnect to the mother's heartbeat of love.

Sometimes the infant's needs were not met in the womb, or the birth experience was traumatic. As a consequence, when the baby is placed on the mother's belly, it may be so disoriented that it has no idea where the mother's breast is. Turning its head from side to side, the baby doesn't know what direction to move in. It cannot move toward the mother's breast and cannot reconnect to her heartbeat.

Disorientation caused by prenatal and birth experiences is replicated throughout life in one way or another. You can observe this continued state of disorientation in people who aren't able to find what is nourishing for them in their work and relationships, or for whom life does not feel nourishing. They may be indecisive, make poor decisions, or stay in jobs and relationships that aren't nourishing for them. They may feel disconnected from their own heart and the heart of the ones they love; they may lack a sense of purpose and direction in their lives.

It's not just birth incidents that cause disorientation. The great African healer, Malidoma Somé, wrote that when a child experiences great suffering, their spirit leaves their body and it is "a journey of many days' walking to get it back." This is Somé's way of expressing the painful disorientation he felt as a child when he was taken from his tribal village and placed alone in a European missionary school. Learning the new ways was difficult. When he was finally able to return home, his disorientation continued because he had now lost his connection to the old ways. Neither culture nourished him. Healing came when he discovered his own personal orientation—he re-established a healing connection to his own inner knowing, made stronger by his exposure to two very divergent cultures.

## Natural orientation

It has been shown through practical research with prenates and infants by people like William Emerson, PhD, Ray Castellino, DC, and Wendy McCarty, PhD, that consciousness is present from the time of conception. They have proven how fully aware prenates and babies are.

As an infant, you responded to your environment—both inside the womb as well as to events that happened outside the womb. The energy exchange through resonance with your mother and father set up a field of communication. If your multiple needs were met, including your need for love, safety and a healthy, non-toxic environment, the field was coherent. This coherence naturally supports a coherent orientation to life. If a natural birth process free of trauma followed this pre-natal growth period, you were born with an inherent orientation to life.

Your innate orientation enables you to naturally maintain your direction toward what is nourishing for you, and toward the heartbeat of love in your relationships. You maintain your connection to your felt sense. You are confident in who you are and where you are going, and when you become disoriented you know what you need in order to quickly reorient yourself.

## Heart orientation

Orientation, the fourth Key, is intimately related to the first three Keys: Energy, Resonance and Kinesiology. When you are oriented you readily access information from your kinesthetic sense and your felt sense, which act as your compass, telling you what is right for you and what isn't. Orientation allows you to relax deeply inside because, when oriented, you face toward your higher self and the Divine—the highest frequencies of nourishment and the heart of love.

When I began to balance my clients' energy systems through Acupuncture and Polarity, I learned the importance of being oriented in the present moment from my heart. Through Five Element Acupuncture, I was introduced to the teachings of the ancient Taoists. They understood that the most powerful healing occurs when you, the practitioner, are connected to your heart and when you are connected to your client's heart—in other words, when you are oriented.

Techniques and systems are helpful for focusing your knowledge and attention. A compassionate heart, however, orients you to who you truly are in your essence—beyond all chaos, problems, non-coherent actions and past pain. This inner connection is to your own North Star, which always keeps you aligned in the direction of purpose, meaning and self-healing.

## 100% present

Being oriented involves being 100% present physically, emotionally and mentally. With orientation and presence, you are receptive to the quantum change your body-mind system is ready for.

I remember a client who had been diagnosed with severe dissociative disorder. She had stayed in many mental hospitals, had been given numerous drugs and had consulted, she said, nearly a hundred doctors, psychotherapists and psychiatrists. Her therapist told me, "It will be impossible for you to work with her because she keeps flipping from one personality to another."

Slowly and gently I asked permission to muscle check for her. Muscle checking revealed the first step she needed: to re-establish her sense of orientation. I muscle checked for a modality that would help her resonate with being 100% present in the moment at all four levels—physically, emotionally, mentally, and at what is called the spirit level in Five Element Acupuncture. Once we had completed the modality, her resonance with self-orientation was established and, much to her amazement, she remained in one identity for the balance of the session.

With the Key of Orientation, you keep growing toward your higher vision. No matter what obstacles you have to face, you remain on track in the direction that is most nurturing for you. You are able to set boundaries on non-coherent behaviors in yourself and others. You also maintain your equilibrium in stressful situations, while being alert for genuine threats of danger.

## Orienting to yourself

The first step in maintaining your orientation to life is to know how to recognize when you have become disoriented. Here are a few signs of disorientation:

### *Disoriented Actions*

- You rush from one action or project to another without being able to slow down or prioritize.

- You need drugs, alcohol, cigarettes, coffee, sugar, food or sex in order to relax, calm down or feel better.

- You talk quickly, unable to listen to others; even if listening, you don't hear what others are saying, or others don't feel heard by you.

- You seek approval from others for everything you do.

### *Disoriented Feelings*

- You feel disconnected from love; you don't feel loved or loving. You feel excluded.

- You feel upset, confused, out of sorts, anxious or insecure.

- You lose confidence in yourself and your ability to create anything new or good in your life.

- You feel overwhelmed or need to sleep excessively.

- You feel emotionally charged: impatient, irritated, and angry or in a panic.

- You feel uncomfortable in social or business situations, or feel anxious about an upcoming event.

- You feel disconnected from your body, spaced out, or vulnerable to the negative thoughts of others.

Once you recognize your own disorientation, you are at your point of choice: you can choose to stay in the downward spiral of your disorientation, or you can choose to spiral up by reorienting yourself to your center of balance and nurturance.

There are many ways to reorient yourself. One of the easiest orientation modalities is the Open-Heart Gesture. Sitting or standing, simply extend and relax your arms at your sides with your palms open and facing upwards. This simple modality realigns the basic energy flow through your heart and the palms of your hands; it anchors you in your body in the present, helping you stay connected to your heart. When complete, notice how you feel.

A student told me she once used this modality when she found herself surrounded by a gang. Spontaneously she went into the Open-Heart Gesture. The gang members looked confused, and suddenly the leader turned away and said, "Let's go." She had maintained her orientation to her heart in the face of potential violence. It appeared that her attackers moved into resonance with the frequency of her open-heart gesture of unconditional love, and their desire to do harm evaporated.

## Orienting to others

Another step toward orientation is to make sure you are oriented in relation to other people. Some people can maintain their natural orientation when they are by themselves, but lose it the moment they are with others. Feeling comfortable, relaxed and confident in groups of people depends on maintaining your orientation within yourself and in relationship at the same time.

Relationships improve when you resonate with trusting and understanding others, when you feel supported and safe in social and group situations, and when you interact from your innate sense of what is most nourishing for you and for them.

When you are disoriented around other people, you can quickly reorient yourself by experimenting with a simple modality called the Thymus Tap. Gently and slowly tap with your fingertips on the center of your upper chest, about two inches below your collarbone. As you tap, smile and slowly nod your head Yes. Dr. John Diamond says this subtle action strengthens your thymus gland and immune system. It has a calming and relaxing effect so you more easily relate to others with confidence.

In one seminar I was teaching, a man complained about how difficult it was to communicate with his adolescent son. As I was teaching the Thymus Tap, I suggested he use it and also nod his head in a Yes gesture with his son. At the next seminar he reported that he had been nodding his head when he was talking with his son, and after a few days his son commented, "Dad, since taking that seminar, you're communicating so much better!"

## Orienting to space

Part of being oriented and 100% present in your body requires being aware of your space. If you look around the room you're in right now, let your felt sense tell you if there is anything that needs to be changed in order for you to feel more comfortable, relaxed and energized. Pay attention to where you are sitting or standing in relation to the windows and doors, to the arrangement of your furniture and to the colors that surround you. Notice any lack of order or harmony that clutters your space and inhibits your energy flow.

When you come into a new room, notice how you feel in the

space and where you would be most comfortable sitting or standing. If you are organizing a social or business meeting, consider what is needed in the space and how each chair is placed, so that all the participants feel oriented, energized and enthusiastic. To be in a space where you feel truly oriented puts you in your power spot—the place that is most energizing for you to stand, sit or sleep.

## Orienting to time

The final aspect of orientation requires the right perception of time. The client who suffered from dissociative disorder needed to reorient to herself, and she also needed a proper orientation to time. She needed to be 100% *in the present moment* rather than in her past where she survived her pain by fragmenting herself. It was no surprise that at the end of her session she smiled and said, "For the first time, I feel so happy."

When you are disoriented, you tend to live in past pain and regrets or exist in a future fantasy of some imaginary happiness. Healing and quantum change happen in the present. If you find yourself disoriented in time, stuck in past events or future fantasies, many modalities, including the ones that follow, may help you reorient yourself in the present moment.

## ORIENTATION IN ACTION

Any time you need to reorient yourself, you can do one of the following three modalities: the Pause; the Thymus Tap; or nodding your head Yes. Deliberately taking a pause in the middle of confusion is one of the most powerful ways to reorient yourself. During an argument, breathe deeply, and calmly set boundaries on the non-coherence by saying, "I need to take a pause." When someone has been talking without giving you a chance to speak, gently interject "Let's take a pause here. I need some time to really hear what you're saying and to share my response."

## 1. Take a pause

- Sit comfortably and close your eyes.

- Breathe slowly and rhythmically through your nose. Expand your ribs and belly as you breathe in. Relax your ribs and belly as you breathe out, pulling them inward with your core muscles.

- Each time you exhale, relax your body from your head down to your feet: relax your face, eyes and jaw; relax your chest and upper back; relax your belly, hips and lower back; let go of any tension in your thighs. Let relaxation flow down through your knees, through your feet and into the earth.

- Feel your feet on the ground; feel yourself energized and supported by the earth beneath your feet.

- When you feel fully supported, bring your awareness to the center of your chest, to your heart center. Breathe in unconditional love. Breathe out unconditional love. Let your heart's magnetic field expand to include the people who are with you right now... your family... someone you have a special love for... someone who is a challenge for you... those who are suffering. Continue to expand this love to include the whole world.

- Notice how it feels when you are 100% present physically, emotionally and mentally.

- When you are ready, slowly open your eyes and reorient to the space you are in. Look around you with relaxed and loving eyes. You have now exercised your point of choice to resonate with Orientation.

## 2. Thymus Tap

- Tap on your chest bone or sternum about one inch below the point where your collarbone meets in the center.

## 3. Nodding Yes

- Slowly nod your head up and down while smiling.

# HIGHLIGHTS

▲ Before you can take in and integrate new information or enjoy the company of others, you need to be oriented and fully present physically, emotionally and mentally.

▲ Orientation to others and to time and space is also important.

▲ Any of the modalities described in this chapter may help when you feel disoriented.

▲ You always have a point of choice to spiral up to orientation and self-empowerment.

▲ Using the Key of Orientation is one way to spiral up to greater coherence and orientation.

~~~~

≈≈≈

# PROBLEMS INTO OPPORTUNITIES

≈≈≈

*A problem is something we have and don't want,*

*or something we don't have and want.*

*The external situation is not the problem;*

*our resonance with our own life-depleting patterns*

*is the problem. The gift of every problem*

*is that it offers us the opportunity to change our resonance*

*with these unconscious patterns*

*and make a quantum leap*

*to the next phase of our growth and evolution.*

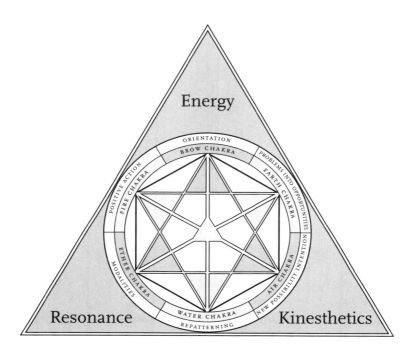

Energy

Resonance    Kinesthetics

ORIENTATION
BROW CHAKRA
PROBLEMS INTO OPPORTUNITIES
POSITIVE ACTION
FIRE CHAKRA
EARTH CHAKRA
NEW POSSIBILITY INTENTION
AIR CHAKRA
ETHER CHAKRA
MODALITIES
WATER CHAKRA
REPATTERNING

ENERGY
RESONANCE
KINESTHETICS
ORIENTATION
**PROBLEMS**
INTENTIONS
REPATTERNING
MODALITIES
ACTION

# KEY 5

~~~

*Underneath every problem is an empowering truth.*

The client, Mary, whose business relationship was threatened by her angry outbursts, originally introduced herself by saying she had a problem with her business partner. Her anger, she said, was caused by her partner's inflexibility and his desire to do things in his own way. Knowing that problems are seldom what we think they are, the practitioner was interested to see what would unfold in Mary's case. Any problem—whether pain, depression, sickness or emotional turmoil—is a signal that your life energy has derailed. The problem is resolved when you discover its power to put you back on track toward the opportunity to manifest what is more true, right and coherent for you.

When you have a problem, you know there is non-coherence in your energy frequencies: you are *resonating* with non-coherent frequency patterns. As in Mary's case, the old pattern takes over and you lose your orientation as well as a felt sense of your needs in any situation.

You might think your personal symptom of distress is the problem. It isn't. Any symptom signals the real problem, which is the non-coherent pattern in your database that you resonate

75

with. This negative resonance causes your symptom and stops you from going into coherent action to resolve the situation. The solution isn't about removing your symptom of distress, which is like disconnecting the wire when a red light is blinking on your dashboard. The solution is to open up the hood and correct the underlying cause—your negative resonance patterns.

## Problems and their structure

A few years ago, an independent pilot research study was conducted with a small group of Resonance Repatterning practitioners and a randomly selected group of their clients. The clients responded to a series of questions about what had motivated them to have a session and whether the sessions they received had made a noticeable difference for them.

The most common answers to the first question: they were suffering emotional pain or struggling with a problem relationship or they wanted something more in their work and finances. Like Mary, they were motivated by their problems to create some kind of positive change.

The results were exciting. Regardless of the problem people brought to their session, 95% of the participants said they felt "better to a lot better" by the end of their session. Once the underlying structure of their problems was identified and their resonance transformed, a new sense of purpose emerged.

One reason our problems may stay firmly in place is that we have a whole story woven around what our problem is and who or what the cause of our problem is. Often we want someone else to agree with our point of view or we want others to make us feel better. The fact is that every problem has a message for us about something we are resonating with that needs to be resolved.

Your problem is an opportunity for learning and growth. The purpose of Resonance Repatterning sessions is to reveal the underlying structure of the problem you resonate with so you can change your problem to something positive. As a result, you can recognize and act on the opportunity in every problem you face.

Using any of the following five steps may help you begin to deal with your problems in a different way.

## 1. *Recognize your problem*

Your problem is something you have and don't want, or something you want and don't have. The first step is to be aware, when you find yourself spiraling down into self-defeating thoughts, feelings, actions or behaviors, that you have a problem.

Mary didn't want to have her temper tantrums any longer; she recognized they were harmful and she hated the pain she was causing herself and her partner. That recognition was her motivation to begin the road to healing.

## 2. *Face your resistance*

We all know people who are not happy in a particular situation, with the state of their health or with a habit they cannot overcome. They genuinely want quantum change in their lives, but their inner resistance shows up. No matter what helpful suggestions you give, they continue to indulge in harmful emotions and detrimental behaviors, and they usually blame others for their problems. Besides blaming and criticizing others, the most difficult resistance to overcome is when someone feels that the situation they are in is hopeless and there is nothing they can do to change it.

What opens the window of hope is to face the problem and assert: "Yes, I choose to find the opportunity in this problem." Genuine willingness is a significant step. It signals that you are taking personal responsibility. Instead of blaming yourself, others, life or God, you are ready to put in whatever effort is required of you. Your proactive response is what makes you receptive to the change you seek.

Mary committed to a number of sessions and used the results to work toward further improvement with her partner. She was no longer blaming him or her customers for her own behavior; in fact, with her new willingness she was able to actively engage her business partner in finding creative solutions for them both.

### 3. Know the components

Remember that problems are held as *non-coherent frequency patterns* within your body-mind system. Life is energy in motion. When you *unconsciously resonate* with unresolved memory imprints, it blocks the natural movement of your energy. The memory imprint is created from the following: the unconscious pain of your earlier needs not being met; a highly charged emotional response; the non-coherent image associated with your unmet need; and the negative beliefs about yourself, others and life that you unconsciously formed.

*Muscle checking* within the context of this Key will take you to all the components that block your energy flow. It will tell you where your unconscious resonance keeps you stuck in pain or in self-imposed limitation from your past.

With Resonance Repatterning you don't need to relive the earlier experience or even retell the story. The past story is locked in place, not by details but by the charged emotion and painful image associated with the unmet need, and by the outdated beliefs you continue to resonate with. When you transform your resonance with the components of your problem, you are no longer the victim. Through muscle checking, the unknown resonance becomes known and can therefore be changed.

Your body-mind wants the truth; you can be energized just by knowing and understanding the truth of the resonance patterns that underlie your problems. This kind of truth always brings a sense of relief. Resolution occurs when you transform your long-held resonance with the frequencies you have unknowingly stored in your database. In some instances, this resolution occurs in one session; at other times, it takes a number of sessions to clear the layers of deeply embedded patterns you resonate with.

### 4. Understand your resonance

The problem is never what you think it is. Encoded in your frequency database is the deeply unconscious rumbling of a much earlier unresolved situation. Every problem in the present is a signal that your body-mind system is demanding resolution of the past, and that your resonance with beliefs and feelings associated with the past experience is blocking the flow of your energy in the present.

One of the components that anchors a problem in place is your lack of resonance with a *life need* for safety, warmth, welcome, bonding, etc., that went unmet in the womb, at birth or in childhood. Mary's "aha," her new understanding, came when she discovered that she resonated with her temper tantrums and did not resonate with the need for safety; she was therefore unconsciously locked into the frequency of the very thing that kept her business relationship in a state of distress.

The purpose and motivational power behind every problem you have is to encourage you to transform your resonance with non-coherent perceptions imprinted from the past; to resonate with being nourished by the positive in every experience, past and present; to resonate with the higher lesson each problem holds for you; and to move closer to manifesting the essence of who you really are in the present.

## 5. Find the opportunity

Your body-mind system knows what your optimal new possibility is. Muscle checking in the Resonance Repatterning system is a way to accurately identify the opportunity behind each problem. Your new opportunity is more than a linear resolution; it is a leap to something better—to a higher state of empowerment and purpose. Your linear resolution might be to go from anger to non-anger or from disease to health, which is certainly a highly beneficial outcome. However, when you no longer resonate with the limitations behind your anger or poor health, your quantum leap might take you into an entirely new realm of possibility.

Quantum leaps don't always follow in the wake of a desired outcome; sometimes they initiate a desired outcome. Mac was a successful businessman who had survived surgery for a ruptured aorta. Six months after his surgery, his blood pressure once more soared to 210/190, and no medication would bring it down. At this point he came to see me, making the purpose of his visit absolutely clear: "I'm only here for my blood pressure —nothing else."

His first session was unremarkable, and when he came for his second session there appeared to be no improvement: his blood pressure remained dangerously high. Muscle checking indicated he needed to share some positive change that had occurred since his first session. He insisted there had been no positive change. As the muscle checking continued to indicate we could not proceed with the session, I asked if he had experienced something positive in any other area of his life, unrelated to his health issue.

Finally he looked up with a puzzled expression and said, "You know, there is something. Last week, I woke up and looked at my wife with love for the first time in our married life. I felt this strange, warm feeling in my heart. It was the first time I had seen her with love rather than with sexual desire. And what's interesting is that this week my wife and daughter keep saying that I am different."

## Levels of healing

This was Mac's quantum leap. Before his outcome—a normalized blood pressure—could manifest, his heart needed to open to love. His quantum leap had changed him in ways he did not at first recognize. But the way he saw life and the way he related to his family had changed, and the difference was apparent to all of them.

When we continued Mac's session, we uncovered the unresolved childhood trauma he still resonated with and his unacknowledged rage at his father's beatings. Once he shifted his resonance with these memory imprints, charged feelings and the traumatic images involved, his blood pressure immediately returned to normal and he achieved the healthy outcome that had originally brought him in for his sessions.

The body-mind wants to know the true problem within

ourselves; it wants resolution of a negative resonance pattern and a quantum leap to the next phase of our growth—in Mac's case, the opening of his heart to love.

Sometimes the outcomes that motivate you to have sessions are only realized slowly, after many sessions. Sometimes the desired outcome may not be realized at all, like the woman with heart failure whose pulses Yeshi Dhonden read. However, the quantum change in who you are, how you live and how you relate to others always takes place. The patient with heart failure was deeply touched when connected to the serenity of her spirit. Mac's heart on the frequency level was healed by opening to love. In big ways or small, some kind of quantum leap occurs each time a problem is truly resolved.

## Openness

As Mac's story illustrates, once the internal structure of our problem is understood and our resonance transformed, we are open for much more of what life offers.

The Key of Problems into Opportunities lets us know there is no reason to remain victimized by our problems. Once we transform our resonance with what underlies our problems, our attitude to life changes, we honor our needs, and often our symptoms of distress evaporate naturally.

# PROBLEMS IN ACTION

One of the reasons problems remain anchored in place is that we do not resonate with life needs that long ago went unmet. Getting in touch with your real needs may seem hard, especially if you were taught that they weren't important or that other people's needs come first or if you survived by not having needs. You may not even know what a basic life need is, or how to recognize when it is not being met, or how to express your need in a way that it will be met.

Needs are motivators that support coherent actions and relationships. It helps to have a tool and a system for recognizing the unconscious needs that are associated with every problem.

In the following activity, you assemble an initial vocabulary of needs, and through your felt sense you will begin to recognize the link these needs have with a specific problem you may be facing today. They might be needs that serve your physical body or needs that feed your mind and spirit. With your felt sense you will select a modality for moving into resonance with your need.

You may want further sessions to resolve the problem you are facing, but this introduction to basic needs will take you in the direction of understanding and resolution.

1.  Tune in to a problem you are facing now. Write it down as a negative statement.

2. Below are two brief lists of needs that, when met, bring you a sense of coherence and well-being. Scan through the lists using your felt sense to find the one you feel is linked with your problem. When your felt sense picks what you need, you may suddenly feel relieved or take a deep breath or even feel sad, angry or overwhelmed. Just observe your responses, breathe deeply and accept your feeling and what your body-mind system is sharing with you.

### BASIC LIFE NEEDS

Bonding—Closeness—Harmony

Nurturing—Security—Trust—Sleep

Protection—Boundaries—Positive Touch

Appreciation—Respect—Being Understood

Space—Light—Play—Laughter

### SPIRIT LEVEL NEEDS

Beauty—Gratitude—Peace

Devotion—Compassion—Courage

Creativity—Limitlessness—Radiance

Truth—Unconditional Love—Unity

Wisdom—Meaning—Stillness

3.  When you have a sense of the need associated with your problem, imagine that you are tuning in to the frequencies and the feeling this need gives you. It's a need that right now you do not resonate with in terms of your present problem; but it is a need you need to resonate with. Enhance your resonance with its qualities by using one of the modalities that follow.

4.  Use your felt sense to select an energizing modality or a soothing modality—the one that will enable you to resonate with the quality of your need and begin to bring that need actively into your life to help resolve your problem.

## Energizing modalities

- Put on some rhythmic music and move your hips in a figure-8 pattern. Let every part of your body follow along with the music and this movement.

- Laugh aloud, even if it feels a little strange. Take a deep breath and let out strong belly laughs—"Ha! Ha! Ha!"—until you are laughing on your own.

- With your feet shoulder-width apart, toes pointing forward, bend your knees and begin to bounce up and down. Relax and feel every joint in your body bouncing and letting go. When complete, you may feel energy tingling throughout your body.

## Soothing modalities

- Tone a note using the vowel sound of "eeee."

- Be aware of what you appreciate about yourself, your gifts and good qualities, or the good you have contributed to another. Breathe this appreciation in and say, "Thank you for all you have given me."

- Remove glasses or contact lenses, if you wear them. Look straight ahead, gently blinking your eyes. Relax your eyes until you can effortlessly see 180 degrees around you. You aren't focusing on any particular detail; just see everything. This soft-focus vision activates your parasympathetic nervous system for deep relaxation, for connecting to your feelings and for bonding in your relationships; it also brings a broad, global perspective.

5.  After using your chosen modality to help your body-mind system come into resonance with the need underlying your problem, allow yourself for the next few hours or more to gently internalize the feeling quality of your need. You have strengthened your resonance with the frequencies of this life-supporting need, so you may now notice ways in which this need is met spontaneously by yourself or by the person or people involved with your problem.

Notice if your problem changes or if your response to your problem changes during the day. You may find that the problem simply dissolves. You may find that a quantum leap opportunity appears. Resonating with genuine needs is one important step toward resolving your problems.

# HIGHLIGHTS

▲ Problems are seldom what they seem; they're based on old disordered patterns caused by unmet needs, by highly charged feelings and images, and by limiting beliefs.

▲ Resonance with non-coherent frequencies in your unconscious database can be accessed with muscle checking to make the exact structure of your problems known and to shift your resonance to something new, positive and coherent.

▲ All problems hold the opportunity for quantum change and positive outcomes.

▲ In Resonance Repatterning sessions, you resolve your resonance with all components of the problem and move into the opportunity every problem holds for you.

▲ You do not need to re-experience the earlier trauma related to your present problem.

▲ Once you have diffused your resonance with a problem and its associated unmet needs, you can create a new resonance —one that propels you toward a higher state of empowerment and purpose.

~~~

# INTENTION
# AND THE GROWING EDGE

~~~

*Intention aligns subatomic particles in a specific direction.*

*When we resonate with an intention*

*we become receptive to the unified field—*

*to a reality that may not generally be available to us—*

*which makes manifesting our intention possible.*

*Whatever is not aligned with our intention*

*emerges over time to be resolved,*

*which takes us to our growing edge.*

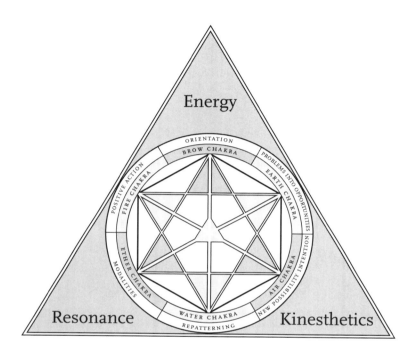

ENERGY
RESONANCE
KINESTHETICS
ORIENTATION
PROBLEMS
**INTENTIONS**
REPATTERNING
MODALITIES
ACTION

# KEY 6

~~~

*All great outcomes begin with intention.*

I am always reminded of Mahatma Gandhi when I think of the power of intention used for a higher purpose. Gandhi taught that "you must be the change you wish to see in the world." His desired change and intention was to bring about his country's freedom from British rule using only non-violent words and actions.

Gandhi encouraged people by his own example to resist with non-violent actions the British decree that Indians must purchase cloth imported from mills in England. Gandhi and his followers took up spinning thread and weaving homespun fabrics so they would no longer need to purchase imported cloth. He demonstrated non-violence through his words, his speeches and in his every action; he mastered the art of non-violent confrontation and taught it to millions of Indian citizens.

Gandhi held tenaciously to his intention for forty years, until at midnight on 15 August 1947 India became a sovereign nation. Because he resonated with actions that were consistent with his intention, this one man led his people to freedom and acquired enduring respect and love.

## Creating anew

Scientific research proves that focused intention moves sub-atomic particles. Coherent intention focuses your mind and creates an ordered pattern at the quantum level. The ordered pattern emits sound and light frequencies that create a magnetic field of attraction. This process enables you to access the vast sea of potential within—the unified field, the energy matrix —which makes quantum change possible.

The Key of Intention is ultimately dependent on the Key of Resonance. You may organize your energy, thoughts and actions around a particular goal, but if you don't resonate with your intention there's little chance your subatomic particles will be aligned enough to attract the outcome you want, no matter how persistently you repeat your positive affirmation or focus on what you want.

Popular self-help programs and coaching techniques emphasize the importance of positive intentions. They recommend that you organize the power of your mind by using intention as a tool to get what you want. They suggest that you make a list of your intentions, divide them into manageable step-by-step actions, and work with them every day. It sounds easy when they teach it. But there are certain steps based on the principle of resonance that would make any self-help program and coaching technique more effective.

Since little in life is accomplished without the motivating power of desire and intention, let's take a closer look at the differences between these two urges.

## Desire

Desire is disparaged in nearly every spiritual tradition because achieving our desires does not lead to lasting happiness. Without understanding what motivates our desires, we can get caught on the treadmill of addiction to wanting things—food, shopping, parties, status, drugs, alcohol, and more. Once on this treadmill, we override our kinesthetic sense and lose our focus on what is most important to us. This makes us vulnerable to being easily manipulated by our friends, family and the media to meet their desires.

The importance of desire is that it's a messenger: behind most desires is an unmet need that seeks resolution. For instance, your desire for junk food may be a substitute for a need you don't resonate with, such as more energy, security or love. These genuine, life-supporting needs are what you want to resonate with, rather than with a list of unending desires.

## Intention

If you find yourself caught up in endless desires, stop and ask yourself what need underlies your desire. Is it a need for connection, safety, independence, meaning, nurturing, or some other life need or spirit level need? Once you identify the actual need your desire is a substitute for, you can use this need to create your intention.

Intention is different from desire. Intention, rather than being a substitute for an unmet need, is like an arrow pointing straight to the fulfillment of your underlying need.

I sometimes find myself ordering clothes from a catalog and then returning them a couple of weeks later. When I pause and take a look at this behavior, I muscle check that my *desire* for choosing and ordering clothes is actually a temporary substitute for relaxation. Once I realize what my real *need* is, I create an *intention* and move into resonance with taking time out during

my workday to relax. This may sound simple, but once I resonate with my intention, the desire dissolves and I find myself
at my next growing edge, which is about creating more time for
myself to do what is most relaxing for me.

When you set an intention for creating anything new in
your life, five essential steps are involved for achieving it: create
a clear vision; know your compelling need; move into an action
that resonates with your intention; enjoy your growing edge; be
aware of your quantum leap. Resonating with each of these
steps supports the achievement of your intentions.

## 1. Create a clear vision

There was nothing wishy-washy or vague about Mahatma
Gandhi's vision of freedom. It was an idea that grew in him
until over time it became crystal clear in his mind—and in his
heart. He created a compelling field of attraction for his vision;
and through the intentions he resonated with, he transmitted
his vision of freedom to others. As a result he drew people to him
by the hundreds of thousands; together, all resonating with the
same clear vision, they became the change they wished to see.

You have to be clear about what you envision. Then through
your resonance with the intentions that support your vision,
you create a magnetic field of attraction. The strength of your
magnetic field is what motivates you to go into action.

## 2. Know your compelling need

Whereas all problems are based on resonance with a need that
was *not* met, every intention is based on resonance with a need
that *is* met.

Your desire for a big house, for example, may be a temporary substitute for an unconscious need for respect, which you don't resonate with. This means that even if you get your big house, your lack of resonance with that compelling need for respect hasn't changed and you still don't feel respected. Once you recognize your need, you can turn it into an intention, in this case "I am respected." When you resonate with being respected, you won't need to buy a big house to gain respect.

The compelling need you resonate with has a frequency that fuels both your magnetic field of attraction and your passion. Unless you resonate with your need, it is unlikely that you will create a strong enough field to meet your need—in our example, the need for respect. The compelling need you resonate with, your passion, the vibratory qualities associated with your intention, combine to create a magnetic field of attraction that manifests your vision from the unified field.

Martin Luther King resonated with the principles of non-violent action that Mahatma Gandhi modeled, and applied them passionately toward attaining racial justice and equality for black people in the US. His compelling need was for equality, value and respect.

When Dr. King climbed the steps of the Lincoln Memorial in 1963 and delivered his "I have a dream" speech to thousands of civil rights marchers, he was so aligned with the need for justice that his oratory won over millions of people, including President John F. Kennedy. His speech reverberates even today as one of the most inspirational ever made, and its catalyzing effect led to the passage of the Civil Rights Act of 1964.

You can wish for justice, you can desire a big house, you can ask for more money, but if your heart's passion is not aligned with the frequencies of the underlying needs that these things represent, you are not likely to achieve them. Without resonance you won't be convincing to yourself or to others. Martin Luther King painted a picture of justice so persuasive that people could see and feel the need for it. They passionately committed to its achievement, regardless of the personal price many had to pay.

### 3. Move into action

Mahatma Gandhi was so committed to his country's independence that he exchanged his European clothing for simple homespun garments. He taught himself to spin yarn, and his nonviolent actions against the British decrees became a symbol for his country's freedom. He taught his followers the art of peaceful civil disobedience and led them into demonstrations that caught the world's attention. All his actions, and the magnetic field of his own radiance, inspired and changed those who came in contact with him.

The success of your intention depends on your resonance with a clear vision, with a motivating need, with your passion to meet your need, and with the actions required to put the intention into motion. Without coherent action, intention leads nowhere. If Martin Luther King had simply practiced his speeches in his living room, he would never have been a catalyst for the kind of change he initiated.

The action that corresponds to your intention creates a vibration, which similar frequencies in the unified field respond to. The resonating frequencies vibrate back and forth as they do between the vibrating tines of tuning forks. The result of this energy exchange is that you begin to experience the vibratory qualities of your intention. Outcomes follow, often in unexpected ways.

## 4. *Enjoy your growing edge*

When you create an intention and resonate with it, gradually all non-coherent frequencies that are not aligned with your intention will emerge to be transformed. Intention by its nature leads to personal transformation. Every positive intention carries a responsibility to honor your innate need for growth toward more unity, harmony, creativity, health and self-actualization.

Resolving the non-coherence within yourself that is not aligned with your intention brings you to your growing edge—to the place of your fearful or angry projections, to your sense of inadequacy, or to hopelessness when obstacles seem insurmountable. In his quest for his country's freedom, Gandhi had to face every obstacle within himself—all the shadows that might have eclipsed his radiance—during the forty years he served as a moral compass for his country and the world.

The more you are able to transform your resonance with the frequencies that limit you, the more energy becomes available for achieving your intentions and your vision. Appreciate your challenges, because personal transformation—physical, emotional, mental or spiritual—is inevitable as you move to your next growing edge.

In a seminar some years ago I was teaching about the power of resonating with intention, and a student enthusiastically spoke up, expressing her very clear intention: "I want unconditional love in my relationships."

I responded by asking: Are you sure? To truly resonate with unconditional love, you will be led on a life journey—the path of the warrior. Coming into resonance with this intention means you are willing to transform everything that is not unconditional love. You will need to align all your actions in the direction of

97

love, even with those growing-edge places and memories that seem the opposite of love. She was silent for a moment. Then, with a little less bravado she said: "Yes, I still want unconditional love."

It is easy to say "I want this, I want that" and forget there is a responsibility that accompanies our positive intentions. Intention, unlike desire, is about growth and personal transformation. Any unresolved emotion or limiting belief—even from our family's generational history—will surface to be healed and to contribute to our continuing growth.

## 5. Be aware of your quantum leap

When you resonate with every aspect of your intention—with its vision, its compelling need and its action steps—and when you transform your resonance with any obstacle that arises, you create a force field of resonance that attracts matching and harmonious frequencies. Be open and receptive. You may be amazed by what transpires: the outcome might be exactly what you intended, or it might be something different from what you intended—a quantum leap.

A quantum leap is not something you consciously decide to do or put in efforts to achieve. A quantum leap is when you move from one state to another with no transition in between. There is an element of surprise, even a sense of grace, as something unexpected opens up within you or in your life.

Martin Luther King, a Baptist minister, set out to achieve equality of seating for black people on the Alabama bus system. His unexpected outcome and his quantum leap was that he become the leader of the Civil Rights Movement, was recognized internationally and was awarded the Nobel Peace Prize.

## Willing partner

You are an energy being comprised of vibrating frequencies, living in an ocean of energy. Your focused intention aligns frequencies in the direction of your choice. As a result of your willingness to resonate with every aspect of your intention, the ocean of energy partners you, offering every opportunity for your growth and evolution, even if the intention itself remains unmanifested.

Our commitment is to resonate with our vision and intentions and to go into coherent action to manifest them. The final outcome is not in our hands. Whatever the outcome, the journey always leads to personal transformation.

## INTENTION IN ACTION

For some of us, the minute we state an intention, an immediate negative projection appears. For example, you might say "I'd like to take this new seminar." Your negative projection pops up with a red flag that says "It's too difficult! I can't afford it. I'll have to drive too far. I don't like groups"—and the list of projections goes on.

How many times have the negative projections you resonate with talked you out of a great opportunity before you even got started? The truth is you will gain far more benefit by living from intention and by changing your resonance with non-coherent projections, than by not getting started at all.

Think of an intention that fulfills a need you have

right now. Here are four antidotes when negative projections appear. Take your time to try them all, and use your felt sense to select the modality that will strengthen your resonance with your positive intention.

## Four antidotes

1. In place of negative projections, focus on positive projections instead. For instance, "I take this class and gain a new understanding that meets my need for (choose a phrase like: personal growth, helping my family, effectiveness, etc.)." Now you are creating a field of attraction and organizing your subatomic particles in a way that brings your goal closer to fruition.

   Rather than live your life from what you don't want, live your life from what you do want. In this way, you set up an exchange of energy based on unconditional love for yourself and others.

2. Commit to yourself by understanding both the benefits and the consequences of your positive intention. Say: "I am willing to accept the consequences of manifesting my coherent intention." This gives you an opportunity to imagine and accept the changes that might occur in your life and how you might be different when your intention manifests; it also gives you an opportunity to fine-tune any aspect of your intention. If negative projections appear at this point, acknowledge them and replace them with a reminder

of your positive projections. Negative projections are simply one aspect of your growing edge.

3. Determine the positive actions that will help you achieve your intention. What steps are needed, what skills and resources do you need, in order to realize your intention? Make a list of these steps. Using your felt sense, you will pick the modality that moves you in the direction of your intention, regardless of any obstacle you might encounter on the way.

4. A great statement to resonate with is: "I move into action toward my intention with purpose, patience, inner strength, drive and integrity." With your felt sense, choose a modality from the short list that follows to start the process of resonating with this statement, as well as with your positive intention, your positive projection and your positive actions.

## Energizing modalities

- Drumming: If no drum is available, drum on a chair, a saucepan, a table, a book or on your own legs or even your body. Have fun. If possible have other people join in.

- Stretching: Yawn and stretch every part of your body, making loud, uninhibited noises as you do so.

- Energy Contact: Place your right middle finger under the base of your spine at your coccyx and your left index finger at the top of your spine in the hollow underneath your skull bone. These two points are Polarity contacts that balance your sympathetic nervous system. Gently hold the points, moving your body in any way it wants, until you feel complete.

## Soothing modalities

- Palming: Rub your palms together and then cup them over your closed eyes, with your fingers resting diagonally across your forehead so no light enters. Breathe deeply and relax yourself physically, emotionally and mentally.

- Color: Tune in to a color you need, such as red for stamina; orange for confidence; yellow for vitality and power; green for cleansing, calming and healing; blue for peace and contentment; indigo for inner vision; pink for unconditional love; and violet or white for spiritual receptivity. Use your felt sense to know where your chosen color is needed and then imagine the color at that place—on a specific area of your body, in an internal organ, or surrounding you like an aura.

- Positive touch: Place the pads of your fingers gently on the top of your forehead and bring them slowly down the front of your face, maintaining a soft contact as you do so. Then drop your hands down and rest. Repeat this soothing modality as often as you like.

Your shift in resonance creates a more harmonious field for your personal transformation and for your vision to manifest.

# HIGHLIGHTS

▲ Whatever is accomplished in life is through the motivating power of desire and intention.

▲ Desire is a short-lived substitute that does not meet a life-supporting need; intention points the way toward meeting the need.

▲ Achieving what you *desire* does not necessarily lead to growth, evolution and happiness; achieving what you *intend* always leads to growth, evolution and happiness. It is always transformative.

▲ Intention leads you to your growing edge to resolve everything that is not aligned with your intention.

▲ Resonating with your coherent intention focuses your mind and creates an ordered pattern of subatomic particles.

▲ Your vision, need, intention, passion and action set similar frequencies vibrating in the unified field—the vast sea of potential; or the vast sea of potential sets you vibrating so you become attuned to your vision, need, intention, passion and action. The energy exchange that results makes quantum change possible.

~~~

# REPATTERNING

~~~

*All frequencies are organized in non-coherent (chaotic)*

*and coherent (ordered) frequency patterns.*

*All frequency patterns*

*can be expressed in words and statements*

*and are accessible through Resonance Kinesiology.*

*Identifying specific patterns*

*and transforming our resonance with them*

*is a process we call Repatterning.*

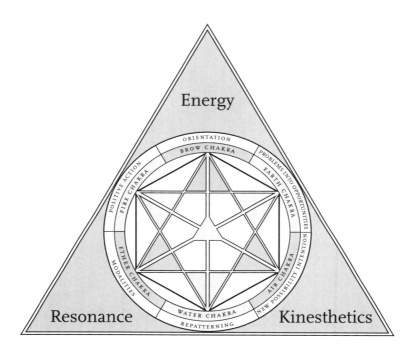

ENERGY
RESONANCE
KINESTHETICS
ORIENTATION
PROBLEMS
INTENTIONS
**REPATTERNING**
MODALITIES
ACTION

# KEY 7

~~~

*Bring your hidden patterns to light.*

A friend told me about an insight she had while walking on a lawn in New England, enjoying a moment of quiet introspection. As she walked, she became aware of different patterns in the grass. One was the simple upright shape with slim blades that she associated with grass. It was soft under her bare feet. The other was a series of radiating clusters with broader blades. When she walked on them the blades were slightly prickly. She was fascinated by the pattern of interlocking pinwheels these prickly blades created. It slowly dawned on her that she was admiring an invasive weed called crabgrass and that the two forms of grass, one soft and the other prickly, were competing for limited space.

When I heard her experience, I realized that the old stories in our database operate much like the prickly crabgrass. Rooted as they are in earlier experiences when our life needs were not met, our negative feelings, unmet needs, non-coherent beliefs and survival perceptions take hold like crabgrass. Our unre-solved patterns are as strong as weeds that grow through cement and survive without water. They compete for our life energy, having all the vitality of our unconscious and highly charged feelings to sustain them.

Underneath our problems and complaints lies a hidden network of old stories and unmet needs. This was the answer, I realized, why healing modalities work for one person and not for another. Removing a patch of crabgrass and planting new seeds of healthy grass might be enough for one person. But with another person, the soil needs to be completely turned and composted in order to support new growth and a healthy lawn.

## Forming patterns

I knew from the work of the Swiss scientist, Dr. Hans Jenny—pioneer of Cymatics, the study of wave phenomena—that sound frequencies form patterns in physical matter. I had watched the films of his experiments in which he placed sand on a metal plate and then vibrated sound through the plate. Like magic, the sand moved into coherent and often beautiful patterns that varied depending on the harmony and amplitude of the sound frequencies he played.

In an equally remarkable experiment, Dr. Guy Manners, who evolved the principles and practices of Cymatic Therapy, asked the Jodrell Bank Observatory in England to record the sound frequency of the deep space Crab Nebulae. He repeated Dr. Jenny's process, using this recorded sound—and the sand on the metal plate vibrated into the shape of the Crab Nebulae!

The vibrating sounds in Dr. Jenny's experiments create both ordered and disordered patterns in physical matter. It became apparent to me in my clinical practice that the vibrations of our thoughts and feelings also form ordered and disordered patterns in the dense matter of our body-mind field. It is these vibrational

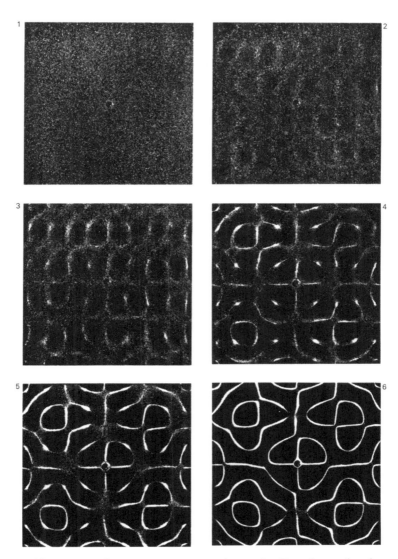

**Visible patterns of resonance.** In an experiment, Dr. Hans Jenny placed a crystal oscillator beneath a steel plate covered with sand. The oscillator played an audible sound vibrating at 7,560 cycles per second, approximately the note of A# at four octaves above middle C. These frequency vibrations were transmitted through the plate to the sand, which responded through resonance to form the clear pattern illustrated above. The longer the coherent sound frequency is played, the clearer the patterns become.
Photos by Hans Peter Widmer and Christiaan Stuten

patterns that determine the perceptions and responses we have to the events in our daily lives.

I further realized that words reflect and create vibrational patterns too. I could therefore translate the vibrational patterns of our perceptions and responses into statements, organize them into categories of coherent and non-coherent patterns, and use them as cues for bringing to light the hidden network of old stories and unresolved issues held in our body-mind field.

## The importance of patterns

It is the patterns you resonate with that make you unique. Some of the patterns serve you well and some of them don't. They reveal themselves in the ways you organize your life, in the quality of your relationships, and in your perception of life's goodness.

Some patterns are archetypal and generational, passed on from your ancestors. Other patterns are formed by your resonance with the physical, emotional and mental qualities associated with your chakra energy centers and your meridian channels.

If your energy, for example, is blocked or non-coherent in your solar plexus chakra—considered to be your seat of power—then you may resonate with a pattern of abusing your power or feeling powerless; of acting aggressively or being on the receiving end of other people's aggression.

Patterns are formed by your perception of yourself, others and life, in response to your experiences from conception to the present. The information in your database is stored by association with similar events and by your responses to those events. Every time something happens to you in the present that is unconsciously perceived as similar to an experience in your past, the past perception and response is superimposed on the present event. Your vibrational pattern, whether positive or negative, is reinforced by repetition, just like the sand patterns in Dr. Jenny's experiments.

## Changing the patterns

When you toss a pebble into a still pond, you see ripples spreading out in all directions. Toss another pebble into the pond and watch what happens. If the ripples match each other where they intersect, the waves are amplified; the pattern, whether positive or negative, gets stronger. If they don't match, they form a chaotic pattern. If the hills and valleys of the ripples are exactly opposite, they cancel each other out.

This is probably how patterns are etched and amplified in our field. And nature gives us a clue here about how to strengthen our coherent patterns and neutralize our non-coherent ones.

For example, you have an opportunity to take on a new assignment at work. You're well qualified for the task and it will mean a promotion once completed. This is a new ripple on your pond. As you approach the task you begin to feel anxious, and for some reason guilty as well. Your anxiety inhibits your usual ability to make good decisions, and your relationship with your staff begins to suffer. You have an older ripple that doesn't match the new ripple and it is creating chaos as you attempt to take on your new role.

Something has to change. You make an appointment with a Resonance Repatterning practitioner who tells you about the non-coherent frequency patterns buried in your unconscious that stop you from moving forward. Because they are unconscious, they can't be unearthed through analysis or by talking. But left undetected and unresolved, they will keep you from achieving

your goal. They are like weeds that push through your unconscious and make themselves known as back pain, an accident,
an argument or a problem at work. Any symptom is a sign that
there are non-coherent frequency patterns needing to be
resolved.

With your practitioner you discover—through muscle checking and the statements delineated in the Resonance Repatterning
manuals—that your underlying problem has nothing to do with
what's happening at work. In this situation, it may have everything to do with an unconscious pattern of loyalty to your family
system. Family system loyalty is an old pattern that is deeply
buried in the ancestral energies of every family. This particular
pattern determines what behavior is required for your "membership" in the family.

In this imaginary case, let's say your family resonates with
"Just this far and no further." Your new assignment at work will
require that you grow and expand beyond the achievement of
any other family member. When you step outside resonance
with your family values, you may find yourself feeling guilty,
anxious or afraid and not know why.

Using the process based on the Nine Keys, you identify a
new pattern of accomplishment that serves both your career
and your family system, and you cancel out your resonance
with your non-coherent family pattern. Instead of guilt you now
resonate with celebrating your new pattern of honoring your
family and achieving your highest potential. You are creating
compatible ripples that intersect to amplify the new pattern.
This new resonance in your family system even gives your children permission to grow and achieve in accordance with their
unique gifts.

## Categories of patterns

Your patterns are like your computer's operating system: they organize stored information. When you have a hunger for more —for spiritual growth, accomplishment, health, creative expression, adventure, self-knowledge—you are getting a signal that an old pattern is ready for an up-grade.

To make both old and new patterns accessible, I have written them down as Repatterning formulas, organized into four major categories: primary and unconscious patterns, chakra-meridian energy patterns, relationship patterns, and vision patterns. In this chapter, I give you some examples of a few of the Repatternings in these categories, and the range of symptoms that can be resolved when resonance is transformed. I'll also give some examples of what happens when Resonance Repatterning is put to use in organizational settings and even with animals.

Not every Repatterning session requires a problem or symptom. In my private practice I also worked with people who were happy and successful. What they loved was receiving continued support to amplify their resonance with good health, a satisfying career and fulfilling relationships. For the same reason, there are students who take and retake the seminars as a way to maintain balance and harmony in their everyday lives, as well as to be with others who also want to integrate a conscious and transformative way of living.

### 1. Primary and Unconscious Patterns

Most non-coherent primary and unconscious patterns are formed in early childhood when we didn't have the resources for resolving the problems and the unmet needs we faced.

Until the age of eight, children have a highly developed right-brain hemisphere—associated with bonding, imagination, creativity and play. After the age of eight, the left-brain hemisphere—associated with speech, linear thinking and analysis—generally begins to develop. This means that younger children rarely express their unmet needs through direct communication and linear speech. They tend to express them symbolically—by withdrawing, getting sick, through behavioral problems, tantrums, whining, bed-wetting and so on.

Because these expressions are symbolic, they aren't recognized by left-brained adults who misunderstand the child's symbolic language. Consequently the child's needs remain unmet, and the unresolved, highly charged feelings, negative beliefs and painful memory images are stored as non-coherent frequency patterns in the body-mind field.

Your unresolved responses to your early childhood experiences determine through resonance how you breathe, hear, see and laugh. They affect your perception of whether life is safe and welcoming, and the way you either move ahead with confidence or hold back. These patterns deeply affect your sense of self-worth. Each pattern, imprinted at an early time in your life, continues to predetermine your responses in the present, both coherent and chaotic.

EARLIER EXPERIENCE REPATTERNING Here's an example of how an unconscious pattern appears in a person's life and how it is transformed.

A client I'll call Olga had an intense and irrational fear of authority, to the extent that her health suffered and she was unable to sleep or eat. An upcoming IRS audit had her in such turmoil that she asked a Resonance Repatterning practitioner for some sessions. Through muscle checking, the practitioner identified that Olga needed the Earlier Experience Repatterning, which went straight to the underlying resonance that caused her fears. With her patterns identified and her resonance with them transformed, Olga writes: "Until my session I didn't realize that my fear in the present was the same fear of authority I had learned as a child. I grew up in Germany during World War II and it was this fear that permeated my entire family."

Olga resonated with a pattern of fear created when there was no one to meet her childhood need for safety. Unresolved, her fear was constantly superimposed on the present and became the overriding theme of her life. When her resonance with the old pattern was transformed and she resonated with her need for safety being met in appropriate ways, her experience of life changed quite dramatically.

She writes, "When a policeman passes me now it doesn't faze me. My son commented that I haven't mentioned the upcoming audit. In fact I've been traveling and am even thinking about dating again."


## 2. Chakra and meridian patterns

The patterns in this category are related to the chakra-meridian energy system. Your energy steps down through each chakra and circulates in a self-regulating fashion through the chakras and the meridian channels. A pattern is established by the way your energy flows through your chakras and channels. If your energy is blocked in its flow physically, emotionally or mentally, it forms non-coherent patterns.

If you have difficulty making decisions, getting projects done, networking, letting go, digesting new ideas, accepting abundance or dealing with sexuality, there is sure to be an imbalanced frequency pattern in one of your chakra centers or meridian channels.

FIVE ELEMENT AND MERIDIAN REPATTERNING  In the following case, a practitioner gives an example of how a physical symptom has both a medical cause and a non-coherent resonance issue holding it in place. The story illustrates the importance of receiving medical treatment along with identifying and resolving the underlying frequency patterns.

"My friend was hospitalized because he suddenly couldn't breathe. The diagnosis was blood clots in his lungs and he was given 15 liters of oxygen every 24 hours. He was quite weak and unable to function. He agreed to a session because, in his own words, 'There is nothing to lose'."

The practitioner discovered an imbalance in the man's Metal Element, which is related to the lung meridian. Muscle checking indicated that he needed to resonate with opening the space for something new by letting go of the pain of his divorce.

"To balance his Metal Element and his lung meridian, he needed to resonate with trust in God, his doctors and the strength of his system to heal his lungs. He also needed to create loving connections with others in the present. His positive action was to hold the meridian point, Lung 9.

"The results were quite dramatic: the next morning his oxygen intake was reduced to 4 liters and, although his doctors had told him he would be hospitalized for three weeks, they said that with his remarkable progress he could go home in three days."


### 3. Relationship patterns

The third group of patterns is about relationship. The best relationships enjoy a balance between giving and receiving, leading and following, bonding and separation. In coherent relationships where bonding is established, we thrive on interdependence: the mutual needs of each person are met, including the needs for self-respect, safety, self-expression, affection, intimacy and space. When needs like these are not met, personality defenses take over and the relationship is marred by reactivity, resistance, co-dependence, fear, control, and non-coherent, often unconscious, competition.

REPATTERNINGS FOR SELF-ACCEPTANCE  In an unusual pilot project, a South African practitioner worked for ten weeks in a prison with a group of women serving life sentences. Many of them had been jailed for killing their husbands. They were all women who had never experienced relationship as a means for connection, safety or intimacy. Most had suffered insurmountable hardships and abuse over and over again. They also had many challenges inside the prison to deal with. The practitioner hoped that through repatterning she could help them heal the past and resonate with love and appreciation for themselves in the present.

She began by giving each one of the twelve women a private Resonance Repatterning session and then continued for two months giving weekly group sessions. After the ten weeks were complete, the practitioner asked the women to write about their experience. One woman wrote, "I was down and felt like I was worthless, but after a few meetings I am a different person. Every negative thought that I had is gone and I'll never go back to who I was. All I can say is that all my friends inside can see the change in me and it makes them positive as well. Everything I now say and do, I do it with a positive attitude."

You can feel the change in resonance this woman has embodied, once the qualities of connection and safety were introduced into her life. Her situation in the prison remained the same as before, but her attitude and response changed. As she empowers herself through her resonance with positive thoughts and a new perception of her self-worth, she benefits herself and, through the unified field, her friends benefit as well.

REPATTERNING FOR BONDING  Many patterns underlie addictions, which impact brainwaves, biochemistry and behavior. In the following story, a practitioner describes one of the patterns that supported her recovery.

"I had multiple addictions and was in such pain over my inability to control them that I became actively suicidal. When a friend told me about this repatterning work and the science behind it, I thought, OK, this is it. This is something I can learn to do for myself.

"There were two significant turning points, both of which came in early sessions with other practitioners. The first eye-opener was the realization that the source of my addictions was my unmet need to reach out and bond with others. Only through drugs, alcohol and caffeine was I able to enjoy relationships with other people. The second realization was that my key to freedom from addiction was to connect with others without the help of any outside stimuli.

"I have now been clean and sober for eight years, and free of nicotine for seven. I'm still working on the caffeine! I have an active professional practice and often see people who are struggling with multiple addictions as I was. In their sessions, the motivating factors behind their addictions always become astoundingly clear. When I can help my clients' resonance change from shame, stigma and resistance to getting the help they need, their recovery begins."

REPATTERNING FOR SHOCK AND TRAUMA In shock or
trauma situations, our self-regulatory system is overwhelmed
by threatening events that are outside the range of usual human
experience. In response to such events, our energy constricts.
The frequencies of the unmet life need for safety, the traumatic
fight-flight memory images and the highly charged feelings
associated with the memory images are stored throughout the
body-mind system. Unresolved and often unconscious, they
may continue to overwhelm us in the present when the slightest hint triggers the old response from the past.

This kind of pattern-and-response complexity was the driving
force behind Mary's uncontrollable temper tantrums. By releasing the original energy constriction and resolving the unmet
needs, feelings, perceptions and imprinted images, people like
Mary who have suffered severe shock and trauma don't have to
continue superimposing the original experience and its trauma
responses on the present.

The following story is a dramatic illustration of the range of
painful symptoms that can follow in the wake of unresolved
trauma. It shows how this practitioner's dedication to her own
self-healing process, through multiple repatterning sessions,
transformed generations' of hidden turmoil and led to her new
role as a Certified Practitioner.

"Depression has a long history in my family. My mother was
chronically on medication. My father, an alcoholic, was always
attempting suicide. We'd have to hide the weapons so he would
not shoot himself, though once he did and survived. I was a
sickly child and remember thinking "How can I just die and get
away from all this?" By my senior year, I was diagnosed with a
bleeding ulcer. My mother's voice rang in my head: "You just
have to stuff your pain." Later I was diagnosed with post-partum

depression, then fibromyalgia, then PTSD (a stress disorder). I had three car accidents, which led to inflammation of the brain. I was filled with pain that traveled around my body and was only able to sleep about an hour each night.

"I was in the hospital when a friend brought me some information about the Resonance Repatterning system. It had helped a friend of hers, maybe it could help me. The day I left the hospital, I went straight to a repatterning practitioner. After just one session my family saw a change come over me: I had a ray of hope! After three sessions, I knew I had to study this system so I could continue the healing work for myself. I loved having the courage to look at the patterns that came up and deal with them, instead of stuffing them away.

"Today my symptoms of anxiety, insomnia and depression are gone. My fibromyalgia is in remission. I'm doing things now that I haven't been able to do in years. I continue to include chiropractic and massage therapy, but it is the Resonance Repatterning work that goes the deepest. Knowing the reason behind my patterns constantly amazes me. Being able to help myself has been the greatest gift."

## 4. Vision patterns

The fourth group of patterns relates to our vision—on the physical, emotional, mental and spirit level. Life is energy in motion. To be and feel most alive requires a sufficient inflow of light, which directly affects our energy level, our ability to move, and how we feel about ourself and others.

MOVEMENT FOR LIFE REPATTERNING  One of the students in a Vision seminar I was teaching found that when she changed her resonance with the way she moved, her vision changed as well. Before the seminar she had to wear her glasses all the time, not only for her vision impairment but also because she would get migraine headaches if she took her glasses off.

The shift came with the "Movement for Life Repatterning," which facilitated her resonance with the freedom to move like a child, releasing her body of constrictive memory imprints. Before doing the Repatterning, she courageously decided to remove her glasses for the first time since childhood. That night, still free of both her glasses and her migraines, she suddenly realized she was able to read the book that was lying on her bed.

This transformation in her vision lasted six months. During that time she shared her extraordinary experience with others. Many people had strong negative reactions: some didn't believe her; others commented that they preferred her with her glasses on; others told her that the change wouldn't last. By the end of six months, her vision had returned to its earlier state. She had let her resonance with other people's negative beliefs inhibit the movement of light energy into her body-mind system.

She was quite philosophical about her loss, realizing that she had an early pattern of giving her power away to other people. She understood that she needed more repatterning in order to resonate with maintaining the strength of her own convictions and with setting clear boundaries.

## Repatterning in organizations

When repatterning is used with consistency in larger settings like businesses, non-profits, prisons, social service agencies, hospitals and schools, it has the power to create meaningful change throughout the organization. You've read about how prison inmates with life sentences shifted their resonance from abuse and violence to the frequencies of appreciation and self-worth.

In another organizational setting—a school—a Certified Resonance Repatterning Practitioner and special education teacher has permission from the school's administration, her kindergarten through high school students and their parents, to provide Resonance Repatterning sessions.

The sessions, she writes, "work immediately with children who have difficulties with vision, hearing, sensory, physical and/ or emotional issues. They also provide long-term resolution at a stage when a child's limbic system and cerebral hemispheres are developing.

"I can tell that the children are separating from their parents' energy field and forming their own distinct vibrational field. In the process the sessions transform old patterns in the family system. I teach them that truth is energizing and non-truth is de-energizing. They can really feel this in their bodies."

In a professional setting, just one Key applied at the right time and place may be all that is needed. This busy special education teacher doesn't have the time to apply all the Keys outlined in this book. But because she has the full range of Repatternings and modalities at her fingertips, she can quickly use muscle checking to identify what the child needs in each situation.

She writes: "One child I'll call Maggie was almost legally blind. She could not say an entire word but had to blend the sound of her words part by part. The other children made fun of her. The day of our session, she was to be in a play and was afraid she'd make a mistake. She was also fearful about upcoming state tests in math and reading.

"Our session included the Memory Imprint Repatterning, which revealed that Maggie carried the imprint of being born in a limousine on the way to the hospital. Her dad wasn't there and her mom was filled with stress and fear about not making it to the hospital. Maggie retained the memory imprint of that stress and fear until we brought it to light and repatterned it. Her new pattern aligned her with the energy of having both parents support her so she could face the future and make it. That day, she was great in the play—she got through all her lines with no mistake. Later that week she scored the highest of the group in the state's reading test."

## Repatterning for animals

People are often amazed that animals need repatterning and respond well to sessions. Like people, animals are energy beings and have a heightened sensitivity to energy and resonance.

In one of my favorite animal stories, a practitioner told of visiting a friend's aviary where he bred and protected exotic birds. He pointed out two birds he was worried about because they belonged to a species on the verge of extinction, and they refused to mate. The practitioner immediately offered to do a session. Before the session was complete, the two birds were happily mating. The man, obviously impressed, commented, "Maybe you'd better do a session on me!"

## Releasing energy flow

Rather than focusing on an event, a problem or an intention, doing a Repatterning focuses on your *resonance* with a particular pattern that underlies your problem—for example, a parental pattern, a compensation pattern, a movement for life pattern. Through muscle checking, only the most relevant aspects of your pattern are identified—free of judgment and with compassion—so the knotted threads of past emotional responses, beliefs and perceptions can be effortlessly untangled. With sufficient order restored in your body-mind field, your energy can express itself more freely.

When you bring your patterns to the light of day and transform your resonance with them, your energy flows more strongly. Much like a stream of water when debris is moved aside, the flow of your own energy brings about balance and promotes self-healing throughout your body-mind system.

## REPATTERNING IN ACTION

In earlier activities you harmonized your life energy for your own well-being. You used the sound of your voice and other modalities to shift your resonance. Now let's use what you have already learned and add to it the Key of Repatterning to create a mini-Repatterning session with a short extract taken from one of the seventy-five Repatterning formulas.

COMPENSATION REPATTERNING  Compensation is a common family and relationship pattern. When unconditional love was perceived as missing in our lives, often through a perception of abuse or neglect, we survived by getting attention from others in any way we could—and we resonate from then on with the absence of unconditional love.

When we resonate with our compensations, we believe that any attention we get has to be earned and that negative attention is better than no attention at all. We learn a compensating behavior that helps us survive, but actually depletes our life energy. It takes over like crabgrass. It becomes the way we relate to everyone and to life. It stops us from being honest and direct, from communicating our need for love, from expressing our loving feelings, and from achieving any real intimacy in our relationships.

Here's a taste of how you might apply the Key of Repatterning to a compensating behavior pattern you may recognize and want to change.

1. Using your felt sense, scan the short list of sample compensation statements below. In the Compensation Repatterning, these words and statements express the non-coherent end of the frequency spectrum. You will either recognize your compensation directly or know it's the right one when you have an "aha" response. If you suddenly feel constricted, sad, angry, or have a physical reaction—tension in your jaw, sweating hands—this may also be a signal for you. Select a statement you relate to, that you feel you resonate with and that you'd like to transform.

- I take care of you so you will love me.
- I withdraw and isolate myself in order to feel safe.
- I agree with you so you will accept me.
- I only feel loved if you give me gifts and money.
- I control you with my anger so I feel safe.
- I need to be right to be loved.
- Only if I excel will you love me.
- You only love me if I am self-sufficient and have no needs of my own.

2. Did you find one you resonate with? Whatever your body response, your felt sense is making itself known. Write the statement down.

3. Underneath every compensating pattern is the need for love. Write down: "I am loved unconditionally, just as I am." Breathe slowly and deeply. Relax from head to toe as you repeat this life-affirming phrase aloud.

4. Now you are in the coherent end of the spectrum. Scan the following statements, paying attention to your felt sense, and find the statement your body-mind system wants for you. These statements represent empowered relationship patterns created when your needs are met in an environment of unconditional love. Select the one that makes you feel uplifted in some way:

   - I am welcomed, loved and accepted in this world.

   - I am empowered to be responsible for myself.

   - I speak from my truth and you still love me.

   - I am loved, and the source of that love is within me.

   - I lovingly set clear boundaries so I feel safe with you.

   - I am open, honest and genuinely myself.

   - I freely give and freely receive.

   - I express my needs and am also loved.

5. Did you smile inside or have any other response when you found your life-enhancing statement? Write down the statement you have just selected. Be aware that the statement you resonate with in #1, and do not resonate with in #4, may not necessarily relate logically to each other.

You have just developed a simple mini-Repatterning with your three statements in #1, #3, and #4:

- A statement that expresses the unwanted frequency of your old pattern (#1)

- The need for unconditional love that was not met in your childhood and that underlies the non-coherent pattern (#3)

- A statement that expresses the frequency of your desired new pattern (#4)

This mini-Compensation Repatterning and the frequency spectrum it represents are uniquely yours. The final step is to select and do a modality that will cancel your resonance with the old pattern and amplify your resonance with the frequencies of your new pattern.

6. Scan the short list of modalities below. You are scanning for a modality that will change your resonance with the old compensating pattern and strengthen your resonance with the new coherent pattern. Write down the modality you select.

Take whatever time you need while doing your modality. Keep in mind that you may need to do more than one, until you have a felt sense of resonance with personal transformation. Perhaps your felt sense will lead you to a modality in an earlier chapter. Trust yourself.

## Energizing modalities

- The Vitality Breath—a quick, vigorous, rhythmic breathing pattern: Exhale forcefully through your nose, vigorously squeezing your stomach in. Relax your belly and you will naturally inhale. Again exhale forcefully through your nose, focusing on exhaling by squeezing your stomach in. You'll create a brisk *out-in* rhythm as you continue this breathing pattern.

- Pulling your toes: With your thumb and index finger, work into the joints of your toes and then vigorously pull each one. Each toe is associated with one of the five major chakras that control the functioning of your body, how you feel and what you think.

- Sing your favorite song out loud.

## Soothing modalities

- The Dolphin Breath: Imagine you are inhaling and exhaling white light through the crown of your head. As you inhale, see the light flowing down your spine. As you exhale, feel light flowing up your spine and out of the top of your head, like a dolphin exhaling through its blowhole. Relax deeply.

- Centering: Place your palms together and bring them in front of your face, your thumbs touching your nose. Breathe deeply, closing your eyes and relaxing. Now bring your hands, palms still together, in front of your heart. Continue breathing and relaxing.

- Acupuncture Point: Called the Palace of Weariness, this is a wonderful point when you are exhausted and need love and a renewed sense of joy and connection with those closest to you. Lightly place your thumb on the palm of your other hand between your index and middle finger just below the web. Breathe deeply as you hold this gentle contact. (This point location is different from ones normally found in acupuncture books.)

7. Take a pause to integrate the modality you have just completed. You have used energy and intention to change your resonance with your compensation, to create a new pattern, and to allow something good in you to emerge. As your energetic frequencies change, you create new neural pathways—even with this simple mini-Repatterning.

8. Reread your three statements. Notice how you feel in response to them. The first statement may hold less of an emotional charge. The second and third may now energize you and give you a sense of relief or perhaps even joy. This tells you that a new neural pathway has been formed and energizing neurotransmitters activated. You are on your way to a more genuine expression of your feelings and needs in your relationships.

# HIGHLIGHTS

▲ Frequency patterns are organized on a spectrum of non-coherent to coherent, both of which define your experience of life.

▲ The Key of Repatterning states that you can shift your resonance from a limiting, non-coherent pattern to a coherent, positive pattern that fuels quantum change.

▲ Each of the seventy-five Repatternings in the Resonance Repatterning system provides a particular formula for going deeply into the source of the problem, efficiently and with compassion, and for releasing the constricted energy that holds the problem in place.

▲ All chaotic and ordered frequency patterns are unique to you.

▲ Using the Key of Repatterning, you have the choice to change the patterns that no longer serve you.

▲ Resonance Repatterning sessions bring your body-mind system into life-enhancing resonance across the full range of human conditions.

~~~

# MODALITIES FOR QUANTUM CHANGE

~~~

*Modalities include all known systems of self-healing.*

*In the Resonance Repatterning system,*

*modalities input energy through sound, light and color,*

*movement, breath, energetic contact and fragrance.*

*These modalities cancel our resonance*

*with non-coherent (chaotic) patterns*

*and amplify our resonance*

*with coherent (ordered) patterns.*

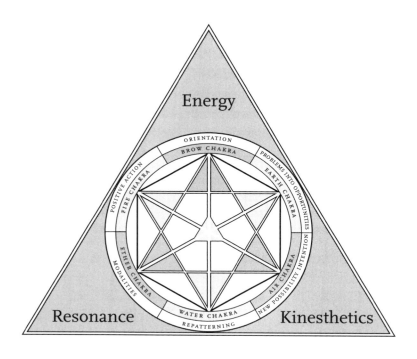

Energy

Resonance

Kinesthetics

ORIENTATION
BROW CHAKRA
PROBLEMS INTO OPPORTUNITIES
EARTH CHAKRA
POSITIVE ACTION
FIRE CHAKRA
AIR CHAKRA
NEW POSSIBILITY INTENTION
ETHER CHAKRA
MODALITIES
WATER CHAKRA
REPATTERNING

ENERGY
RESONANCE
KINESTHETICS
ORIENTATION
PROBLEMS
INTENTIONS
REPATTERNING
MODALITIES
ACTION

# KEY 8

~~~~~~

*Modalities harmonize and balance the flow of energy.*

I love to dance! I've been studying ballroom dancing for some years now and I am always energized by it. Even when I don't dance as well as I would like, my entire body-mind system is still set vibrating. The music dances through me and I experience a heightened sense of coherence that makes all my years of practice worthwhile.

Dancing is an ancient modality found in all cultures around the world. It is an example of how any modality—sound, light and color, movement, breath, touch, fragrance—can spiral you up to a heightened sense of well-being. Any modality can be just as wonderful for you as dancing is for me. When you use the exact modality you need for transforming a negative frequency pattern you resonate with, there is always something about the result that gives you a thrill—a physical uplift, a sigh of relief, a smile of pure joy.

Every time you tone a harmonious sound or wrap yourself in a desired color, whenever you move in a vibrant way or do a balancing energy contact, you are amplifying coherent frequencies in your personal field. In this way, you are using the basic modalities that create and sustain all of life: sound, color and light, movement, breath and energy balancing.

## Activating energies

Every modality inputs harmonious frequencies that vibrate through your body-mind system to create new and ordered patterns. Just as Dr. Jenny vibrated sound through a steel plate to create beautiful geometric patterns in sand and other materials, so energy modalities create the harmonized patterns that become visible in your life as positive change.

Whenever you create a new intention or find the opportunity in a problem, it is the particular modality chosen through muscle checking that changes your resonance and activates the new vibratory pattern in your energy field.

A practitioner told me about applying a modality on the spur of the moment with her two-year-old son, who was irritated and acting out. She muscle checked through a list of energy modalities and found he needed a particular kind of soothing breath. They did the breathing together and he immediately calmed down.

Later her family was caught in rush-hour traffic and her husband, who was driving, became increasingly irritated at the delays. She heard her son say, "Daddy, you need the breathing." The child taught the breath to his father, who also immediately calmed down. The breathing modality, plus the modality of his child's coherence, helped to shift the father's resonance from irritation to calm!

## Choosing the right modality

I've been collecting modalities for over thirty years. I write them down and adapt them so anyone can put them to practical use on a daily basis. When I teach them in seminars, I love knowing these modalities are being used to relieve fatigue in the middle of a workday, to calm an outburst of anger or to help a child. I also love knowing that they are being used around the world to change someone's resonance with a negative pattern.

The most effective and efficient modality is the one that is needed at a particular moment in time for a specific purpose. Such a modality carries the exact frequencies needed to amplify the frequencies of the new, coherent pattern you need to resonate with. Muscle checking allows you to quickly identify the particular modality you need, how much of it you need and for how long. Until you have an opportunity to learn Resonance Kinesiology for yourself, your felt sense will serve as your guide to finding the right modality.

## Amplifying ripples

To illustrate the power of these modalities, let's revisit the image of radiating ripples on a pond. Imagine that you have tossed a stone into the water, and the ripples it creates represent a new frequency pattern you do not yet resonate with.

Now you toss another stone into the water. The ripples of this stone represent a modality you have selected through muscle checking or through your felt sense. It is the best modality for activating your resonance with your new pattern because it is both coherent and harmonically compatible with the ripples of your new pattern. Where the waves meet (constructive interference), the ripples of your new pattern are strengthened, or amplified. Their combined interference makes the waves peak at twice their normal height. Now you have a strong frequency pattern, you resonate with it, and its magnetic frequency radiates through the unified field.

## Modality categories

I have organized hundreds of modalities into categories of sound, color and light, breath, movement, energetic contacts and fragrance. In this way, it is easy to identify the one you need. Even if a modality you have been trained in is not on the list, you can easily add it to the appropriate category. With a full range of ancient and modern modalities, the muscle checking tool allows you to verify that you are using the right one, at the right time and in the way needed by each individual you work with.

### Sound modalities

Sounds made through singing and toning, through harmonic overtones, drumming, gongs, singing bowls and particularly through tuning forks, all amplify coherent frequencies and cancel disharmonious frequencies.

Tuning forks, for example, create a highly coherent sound wave, known as a sine wave. They input a perfectly ordered frequency wave of high-quality energy that has a system-wide effect. Some sound healers believe that the lower the note, or the longer its sine wave, the more healing energy it carries into your body-mind field. Other sound healers work with high frequency sounds to recharge the brain and subtle energy centers.

Two students have reported doing Resonance Repatterning sessions on themselves to identify the pattern underneath the symptom of their painful kidney stones. The doctor in one case was reluctant to sonically break up the kidney stone because of the pain it would cause when the small pieces were eliminated.

The modality both practitioners needed for their individual patterns turned out to be tuning forks. They needed different notes and they needed to move the tuning forks over different areas—one over the pelvis and the other over the kidney area. By muscle checking the exact unconscious pattern, which tuning fork they needed, where it was needed, how to move the tuning fork and how often to use it, their pain was relieved. In one case the student said that after a week her kidney stone was painlessly eliminated. The doctor, looking at her new x-ray, was mystified by its disappearance.

Sound—the Word—is the first phase in the manifestation of the creation. Sound can generate material form and it can also modify form, as seen with the disintegration of the kidney stones. Audible sound vibrates at frequencies between 16 and 20,000 cycles per second (cps) that our ears easily hear as tone and words. This range of audible sound is actually a fairly narrow bandwidth—animals, fish, insects and birds all hear far more subtle (high frequency) sounds than we do.

Inaudible harmonics, which are the overtones of sounds we hear, go way beyond 20,000 cps and are an integral part of harmonic overtoning, an ancient form of healing. The intervals between the harmonics and the high-frequency waves they create carry self-healing properties for positive change at the quantum level.

## Color and light modalities

Forty octaves above the range of audible sound, ultra-high frequency sound emerges as visible color. Your eyes decode these high-frequency vibrations as tint, density, texture, shape and shade. If we use cycles per second as we did with sound frequencies, then dark red is the lowest of the color frequencies, vibrating at about 410 trillion cycles per second. Purple vibrates closer to 750–800 trillion cycles per second. Each color frequency has its related sound—and every sound has its related color.

Colors are associated with the frequencies of the body-mind's energy reservoirs or chakras. The colors of the chakras, from the base of the spine to the crown of the head, progress in the same order as a rainbow: red at the base of the spine, orange at the pelvis, yellow at the solar plexus/stomach, green at the heart center, blue at the throat, indigo at the forehead, and violet at the crown. The frequency of each color matches and supports the frequency of its related chakra. When the chakra is coherent, the colors—to those who can see them—are brilliant; when a chakra is non-coherent, its colors become dull and dark.

Chaotic patterns block the natural flow of your energy through your chakras and meridian channels. The right high-frequency vibrations of color and light can restore the energy flow, just as the right sound or audible frequencies do. The color you need depends on what frequency and modality your particular pattern will entrain with. While there are many ways to apply color modalities, two specific products for color and light have been developed for use in the Resonance Repatterning system.

COLOR FILTER LENSES, worn as wrap-around glasses, are based on the seminal work done by Dr. Darius Dinshaw in the 1930s. Dr. Dinshaw tested the exact combination of frequencies needed for each color to regulate optimal functioning of the body-mind.

To change your resonance with an old pattern, sometimes you need to absorb a specific color frequency through your eyes. This frequency is then transmitted as electrical impulses to your brain and body. Its subtle vibrations may be all that are needed to bring you into resonance with your new pattern and help you create the quality of health and harmony you need.

THE COLOR FILTER TORCH shines the Dinshaw range of color frequencies through a crystal lens, focusing the particular color frequency on a point of energetic contact, such as a Jin Shin point, acupuncture point, vertebra, chakra or a body area.

Each of these contact points helps maintain the balance of your body-mind energy system through the specific functions associated with the particular point. In Resonance Repatterning, the practitioner uses the thirteen Dinshaw color frequencies, with their individual vibrational qualities and functions, to amplify and balance the frequency and function of the selected contact point.

You can also use color as a modality in several very simple ways: by visualizing the color you need and breathing it in; by focusing on a particular color in your environment; or by wrapping a particular part of your body in a color scarf that corresponds to the color you need from one of the chakra or Five Element colors.

In the course of writing this book, Gail and I came to an impasse: we felt pressured for time and that the process of editing and re-editing was never ending. We had lost our sense of excitement. We muscle checked and found we were both resonating with these problems. We also muscle checked that we needed a color modality to change our negative resonance—in this case, we needed to visualize the indigo color of the midnight sky and to see this color inside our head radiating outwards.

After doing this modality, Gail experienced a feeling of expansion, ease, openness—and felt there was infinite time and space available to us. My response to the modality was different:

my posture immediately changed, I found myself breathing slowly and deeply, and I had a sensation of energy pouring down my spine. After this, muscle checking indicated we no longer resonated with our long list of complaints. Our whole attitude had shifted. In addition, our unexpected quantum leap outcome was a refreshing sense of humor and laughter that carried us through the next week of concentrated effort.

Like movement and sound, the use of color for energy balancing is part of every healing tradition around the world. Even as early as 400 BCE Hippocrates, the father of western medicine, used the vibratory frequencies of color and light to balance his patients' body-mind field.

### Movement modalities

Life or energy is always in motion. Movement cannot be separated from energy; movement is synonymous with life. It is an integral part of the kinesthetic sense. Movement creates the shapes and geometry of life, much as wind moves and shapes the clouds. Movement radiates both color and sound frequencies that are beyond the range of what we can see and hear. Itzhak Bentov, in his book *Stalking the Wild Pendulum,* theorizes that even the movement of our hand produces a frequency of sound and light that radiates out to infinity.

Without movement there is no life or learning. It is through feedback between our muscles and nervous system that we decode our sense of movement in space, that we gain a sense of our physical uprightness and our self-orientation. Movement is significant in the self-healing process for maintaining a high level of energy and for improving our ability to learn, grow, transform and achieve our potential.

We all know the benefits of movement as exercise—that it strengthens your heart and stimulates your blood circulation. Soothing or strenuous exercise can relieve stress; it releases endorphins that boost your immune system and gives you a sense of pleasure. Learning new movements promotes neuronal connections in your brain that stimulate intelligence and creativity. Movements like cross-crawls, walking and skipping integrate your brain's right and left hemispheres to improve your focus and access your whole-brain capabilities.

Every movement also has an energetic benefit. The movements in t'ai chi, chi kung and yoga, for example, benefit the physical body as well as the entire body-mind energy field. As a modality, movement has the potential to change how you feel and think, as well as your perception of life.

Every movement, like every thought and feeling, has its own frequency. The frequency of a coherent movement can amplify a positive pattern and neutralize or cancel out a negative one, attuning your body-mind system to more coherent frequency states. The wide range of movements used in the Resonance Repatterning system are chosen because they include the benefits of physical exercise, yet energetically accomplish more than physical exercise does.

KATSUGEN, which originated in Japan, is an inner-directed movement that has helped women give birth free of pain and has enabled opera singers to regain their voice. The practice of Katsugen attunes you to the innate pulsation you need for self-correction, energy balancing and alignment.

SOMATIC MOVEMENTS, developed by Thomas Hanna, PhD, are used in Resonance Repatterning to release the trauma reflex, the ready-for-action reflex and the startle-protective reflex. The core of the central nervous system, the chakra system, and the Governor Vessel in the meridian system are all centered in the spine. Somatic movements create a soft spiraling action through your spine that retrains your brain, relaxes your muscles and releases energy blocks in your body-mind field.

Many other kinds of movements promote high energy levels throughout your body-mind. There are movements that balance your sympathetic and parasympathetic nervous systems. Polarity movements release constriction in all parts of your body. Dozens of eye movements—including up, down and sideways; in circles, squares or spirals; in sharp focus or soft focus—let in more light and release imprinted memory images. When you are out of phase with a project you want to complete or with a person you care about, free movement or dance, with its pulse beat and rhythm, may be just what is needed to bring you back into sync with yourself, what you're doing and the person you're with.

## Breath modalities

At the physical level, breathing is essential for every life function. Slow deep breathing alone has many benefits:

- **Healthy brain** Your brain and eyes need more oxygen to function than any other part of your body. Without oxygen, your brain doesn't function. Many problems with thinking, memory, dementia and Alzheimer's disease may eventually be related in part to inadequate breathing and oxygen deprivation.

- **pH balance** Every time you breathe in oxygen, it alkalizes your system. Every time you exhale carbon dioxide and other gases, you release acidic by-products of cellular metabolism. Since all disease is related to excess acidity, deep breathing alone helps to preserve your alkaline/acid balance and your health.

- **Reduced stress** When you alternate slow deep breathing through the left nostril (exhale then inhale) followed by the same through the right nostril, you synchronize your brainwaves and reduce stress by moving out of your fight-flight sympathetic nervous system responses, into your relaxed, self-healing parasympathetic nervous system.

On the energetic level, breath carries the pranic or chi life energy through your entire body-mind field. Of the many different breathing practices I've gathered, each one offers a unique frequency and input of energy to amplify your new patterns and support physical, emotional and mental health. These breathing techniques can also be used on their own as a modality to create positive change in how you think and feel, and to provide you with a renewed sense of physical vitality.

I've found during my seminars that one of the best ways to maintain everyone's energy is to take a pause four or five times a day and muscle check for a breathing modality we all need. Sometimes we need the Vitality Breath—a vigorous breath that activates the fire center for more energy. Other times we may need the Alternate Nostril Breath—which synchronizes the left- and right-brain hemispheres. When we do a variety of breaths throughout the day, students tell me they have more energy at the end of the day than they did at the beginning. It's the same for me after three days of concentrated teaching.

## Fragrance modalities

As the distilled essence of the plant world, essential oils offer an extraordinary and subtle opportunity to change resonance physically, emotionally and mentally. Each flower, leaf, root and herb has its own refined vibratory frequency. Your sense of smell decodes each frequency and sends a soothing or energizing impulse directly to your emotional limbic brain.

When you feel upset, angry, sad or de-energized, tune in to your felt sense or muscle check for the essential oil you need. You'll find, for example, that peppermint oil may reduce your feeling of depression, or lavender oil may calm you when you feel upset or anxious. Stimulating citrus oils, besides being helpful for cancer, can also help you stay alert on a long drive.

Fragrance offers numerous benefits to the body, emotions and mind. The positive impact on the energy field and physical health makes frequencies from the plant world a powerful resource for self-healing—one that has been used for thousands of years.

### Energetic contacts

Energetic contact always encourages a self-regulatory flow of energy. Every energy-based system, whether Acupuncture, Jin Shin Jyutsu, Cranial-Sacral, Polarity or Reflexology, uses a slightly different map for balancing the body-mind's energy flows. The intent, however, is always the same: to find the blocked energy and restore its pulse and flow.

Resonance Repatterning has the same intent. Because it is both an energy-based and a resonance-based system, it uses some of the energetic contact points from the above systems to balance energy flows by transforming patterns of negative resonance. Resonance Repatterning students learn to muscle check for which modalities will create the frequency input that is needed. In a Resonance Repatterning session you may use tuning forks, color, toning or fragrance applied to the particular energetic contact point—whether that point is derived from the Acupuncture, Jin Shin, Cranial-Sacral, Polarity or Reflexology systems.

When Mary needed to release her resonance with her temper tantrums and childhood trauma, muscle checking indicated a modality of energetic contact. In several of her sessions, she needed to do a Polarity contact on herself, placing her fingers at the top and bottom of her spine, combined with a gentle spiraling somatic movement and the soothing smell of lavender. This combination modality restored the pulse and flow of her blocked energy, and it also released her resonance with her trauma.

## Personal radiance

Each one of us potentially is a modality, as were Dorothy Kerin and Yeshi Dhonden. Achieving a high degree of coherence in your own life means that you have the power to set others vibrating with coherence and self-healing. Just the simple act of smiling or caring for another, or listening with loving, focused attention, may spark another person's upward spiral.

A school teacher I'll call Julie attended a beginning Resonance Repatterning seminar. Shortly after, she received a phone call from a friend whose eight-year-old son had just attempted suicide. It was a recurring problem, but this time the child refused to go to a doctor or psychiatrist. The mother asked Julie if she had learned anything in her seminar that could possibly help.

Julie went over to her friend's house. After getting permission from the child to muscle check for him, she checked through all the Keys to see what the child needed. The only one he needed was the Modality Key. She checked through the list of modalities and came to a sound modality called "Gobbledygook." In this modality you make random nonsense sounds, which activate the right hemisphere of the brain. Soon after starting their gobbledygook sounds, she and the child began to laugh until tears poured down their faces. After a few minutes she muscle checked that the modality and the session were complete.

The next day her friend phoned her. "What did you do?" she asked. "I have my child back! He's playing and singing to himself. I haven't seen him happy like this in ages." While the child may need more help, in that moment the laughter and Julie's loving presence gave him back the happiness he had lost.

People sometimes ask why I've included such a range of modalities in the Resonance Repatterning system. The answer is that everyone resonates differently. If each snowflake is different from all others, certainly the frequency needs and resonance patterns in each person are unique as well. Your system of resonance operates differently from everyone else's. Just the right modality or combination of modalities, at just the right time, in just the right amount, may make all the difference.

## MODALITIES IN ACTION

Throughout this book you've learned a number of modalities and used them to transform your resonance patterns. Here are some additional modalities you can use every day to move your energy into more coherent alignment. You can do these modalities almost anywhere. Keep them in your repertoire and use them when you have a problem or an intention you want to resonate with. You can use your felt sense to select one of the following modalities to do right now.

1. **Sphenoid Cranial Contact** This cranial contact has an emotionally calming effect. Lightly place your index or middle fingers at the corner of your eyes on your temples. You may find your head wanting to move gently. Let this happen. Breathe slowly and deeply.

2. **Zip Ups** This is a classic energy-balancing modality, used in t'ai chi and some of the martial arts. It stimulates the central acupuncture energy channel on the front of your torso. Doing this modality neutralizes any non-coherence you might be exposed to in your environment—such as negative words, images, thoughts and emotions. With the tips of your fingers trace a straight line up the center of your body from your pelvis to just below your lower lip. Your fingers can be several inches away from your body. Repeat several times.

3. **Ear Massage** Your ears are associated with your capacity to hear, with memory, physical balance and with recharging your brain. By placing your thumbs behind your ears and grasping them with your index finger inside the flap, you can gently stretch and press into the sensitive points. You can "unroll" the tops of your ears and pull them slightly downward and upward. By doing this, you are massaging several hundred ear acupuncture points that relate to your entire system. Breathe slowly and deeply as you work into these ear points.

4. **Drink Pure Water** This is an easy and important modality to support your well-being. Many chronic

diseases are related to cell dehydration. Water con-
ducts energy. Every cell is filled with and surrounded
by water and transmits electrical charges that fire
your muscles, heart and every function in your body.
Water detoxifies acid wastes that cause tiredness and
disease. When you drink water, you feel more energized by the coherent modalities you are using
because their balancing frequencies are easily transmitted at the cellular level and throughout your body-
mind system. Drinking pure filtered water is particularly important when you are under stress.

# HIGHLIGHTS

▲ Resonance Repatterning provides a universal range of
modalities—many known and used for centuries and others
of recent origin—for harmonizing the body-mind energy
field.

▲ Each modality is a coherent frequency.

▲ By amplifying coherent frequencies and canceling non-
coherent frequencies, modalities have a harmonizing effect.

▲ With the use of muscle checking, you can select the modality or combination modality you need, the way it is needed,
how much is needed, where and for what purpose.

▲ The right modality is a coherent frequency that amplifies
your new positive patterns so you resonate with them.

▲ Old non-coherent patterns in your database entrain with coherent modality frequencies; the old pattern naturally dissolves and its energy re-emerges as a new pattern, much like Dr. Jenny's sand formations dissolving into chaos and re-emerging as strong, coherent, beautiful patterns.

▲ Modalities create natural entrainment, harmonizing your energy flows and restoring your body-mind system to balance and stability.

~~~~

# POSITIVE ACTION

*Coherent actions we resonate with*

*make us receptive to the unified field of energy*

*through which quantum change becomes a reality.*

*However small the coherent action may be,*

*it has a positive system-wide effect.*

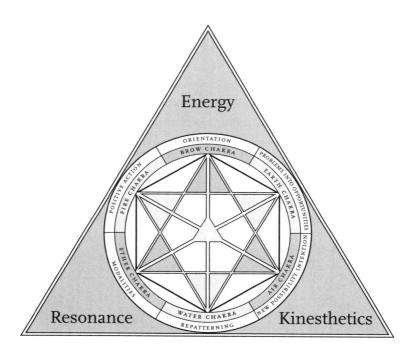

ENERGY
RESONANCE
KINESTHETICS
ORIENTATION
PROBLEMS
INTENTIONS
REPATTERNING
MODALITIES
ACTION

# KEY 9

~~~

*Every coherent action leads to more coherence.*

There's a common experiment in physics in which twin electrons
are spinning in opposite directions as they are meant to. The
surprise is that no matter what the distance between them—
thousands of miles or more—because they are in communication via resonance, they remain synchronized in their spins.
When the spin of one electron is reversed, its partner electron
simultaneously reverses its spin as well. There is no lag time,
no delayed response. The shift is instantaneous.

The spin of these partner electrons illustrates how positive
action takes place. If you've been spinning in a direction that
continually gives you poor results (chaotic patterns), then you
need to change the direction of your spin by changing your
resonance, which automatically causes you to change your
behaviors and actions so they are consistent with your new
coherent patterns. Now when you change the direction of your
spin (your actions), the subatomic particles in your field will
respond just like the spinning electrons in the experiment did—
simultaneously.

Each coherent action you resonate with amplifies your flow
of energy and expands your magnetic field to attract similar

frequencies from the unified field. This is why one coherent action leads to another—and to empowered outcomes.

## Bring it home

Outward change of any kind begins with inner change. Old patterns of despair and self-defeating behavior create well-established unconscious neural pathways in your body-mind system. Every time the old pathways are stimulated by repetitive thoughts, feelings, images and actions, they are fed with proteins that keep the pathways active.

Inner change requires new neural pathways. By activating your resonance with a new coherent pattern or intention, you create new neural pathways. Positive actions then activate the pathways, triggering new connections between dendrites. Every time you feed these new neural pathways through coherent actions and responses, the old neural pathways you once resonated with are weakened through lack of use.

Your goal is to have your new neural pathways take over from the old ones. This means that every thought you have, each word you use, the images you hold onto and every action you take, makes a difference. Resonating with your dreams and ideals naturally helps you go into consistent action toward your dreams. Coherent action constantly activates your new neural pathways so that critical mass is reached and your resonance stays tipped toward permanent change.

There are three different kinds of actions that help you move in a new direction—spontaneous actions, specific actions and strategic actions. To be effective, each one requires your resonance with it. *Spontaneous actions* are automatic and often come as a gift. *Specific actions* are muscle checked from a list in the manuals; they may be only indirectly associated with your session, but are required for maintaining the new pattern and neural pathways. *Strategic actions* are tasks that are directly related to the achievement of your goals.

## 1. *Spontaneous action*

Spontaneous action occurs when you observe, for example, that after doing an activity from this book or having a session, you find yourself behaving differently from the way you did before. Your resonance has shifted at the quantum level and your actions naturally reflect your change in resonance—sometimes in ways that astonish you and sometimes, because it's so natural, in ways you don't even notice.

One cigarette smoker I worked with was not able to stop smoking, even though her doctors had told her she could have a heart attack if she didn't stop. After a few sessions she got in her car and to her surprise she had no desire to light up. In her case, once free of her limiting beliefs and resonance with the patterns causing her addiction, she spontaneously stopped smoking, free of any effort on her part.

Equally, I have seen other cigarette smokers who, after numerous sessions, are still smoking. If spontaneous action does not occur, it points to other layers of patterns waiting to be resolved or perhaps to the need for other kinds of action steps— like attending a Stop Smoking seminar or receiving nutritional support.

## 2. *Specific action*

In one Resonance Repatterning seminar with a group of professional women, each woman was dealing with her own personal issues and needs, as well as seeking clarity on the next step in her career. One woman was interested in pursuing energy work in color and sound, but was having difficulty learning to muscle check on herself, a skill she felt she needed. At one point she volunteered for a demonstration session. Her problem was apprehension about making a career change.

After completing the Parental Repatterning, her positive action was a simple movement from the book *Brain Gym* by Dr. Paul Dennison and Gail Dennison. It was a specific action in relation to her session—the cross-crawl modality. This movement, which integrates the left- and right-brain hemispheres, involves slowly touching the right elbow to the lifted left knee and then the left elbow to the lifted right knee. Rather than doing the modality standing up as was customary, she needed to do it daily for three weeks, lying on her back.

The movement she needed was in fact similar to one an infant makes. As in infancy, its purpose was to integrate her left- and right-brain hemispheres—a developmental stage she had apparently missed in the early part of her life.

At first the movement seemed to have nothing to do with her career change. But in the perfection of her body-mind system, the cross-crawls had everything to do with the change she needed. To be able to muscle check requires whole-brain integration. Like many professionals, she had been educated to use her analytical, linear left brain. It had served her well in the past. However, her new career required that she develop and use her whole brain—her creative, intuitive right brain along with the left-brain hemisphere she was most familiar with.

Had she left the session without this specific action, her energy field and her new neural pathways would not have been able to sustain the change she wanted. She needed a regular input of coherent energy through the specific action, over time, to integrate both brain hemispheres, establish new neural pathways and create an opening for change to occur.

Her small action done consistently over the three-week period made all the difference. She pursued her training in Resonance Repatterning—another consistent positive action—became a Certified Practitioner, applied the work as a consultant in business settings, and finally she helped write this book!

When muscle checking indicates you need a specific action, you know this action is essential for supporting the development of new neural pathways. In the Resonance Repatterning manuals, twenty-seven categories of specific actions provide a large database of options. Coherence muscle checking will indicate the specific action you need. While you may not see the logical connection between the specific action selected and your intention, doing the action always helps sustain your new frequency patterns.

## 3. Strategic action

Resonating with your intentions may lead to *spontaneous actions* —a new way of seeing, perceiving, creating and responding. You may also need specific actions, which may or may not appear to be related to your session. Whether you naturally go into spontaneous action or need a specific action, at some point you will probably need *strategic actions* that you resonate with.

A strategic action is an action or a series of actions that are directly related to your goal. In the example of the cigarette smokers who didn't spontaneously give up smoking after their resonance shifted, the strategic action of attending a Stop Smoking seminar might support the sessions they had received. Their sessions transform their resonance with their real underlying issues, and the continuing strategic action helps to sustain the new neural pathways—which is actually what allows them to enjoy their new resonance with healthy lungs and freedom from addiction.

Strategic actions that you resonate with get you moving in a coherent way. They are the steps you must take in order to create positive change.

The owner of a clothing company in Vancouver was a year into staff expansion when his sales unexpectedly dropped. "I knew," he wrote, "that my staff was scattered and the feeling of synchronicity we once shared had disappeared. I tried different kinds of motivational work to help, but it actually felt like we were digging a deeper hole."

The owner was trying to go into strategic action, but he did not resonate with his goals and the growth of his company, nor did his staff—so nothing helped. At that point he brought in a Resonance Repatterning practitioner to do sessions with his staff and on himself. Spontaneous actions occurred when he discovered a new level of self-confidence in himself as the boss of an expanded staff with a vision of attracting bigger clients. His strategic action was to create a more balanced distribution of responsibilities among his staff.

"Have things ever transformed!" he writes. Within weeks, he received two significantly larger orders which his staff handled effortlessly. Everybody was entrained with each other and with their areas of responsibility, as well as with the company's new vision.

In the corporate world it is taken for granted that growth comes from setting clear statements of mission, vision, values, objectives, strategies and measurable tasks. Extraordinary corporate outcomes increase exponentially when strategic actions are aligned with the Nine Keys and when unconscious patterns of resistance and lack of resonance are removed.

## Effortless and joyful

When your energy is flowing as a result of resonance with coherent patterns, then positive action steps are much more than a long to-do list that you don't resonate with or that you want to be done with as quickly as possible. By synchronizing your needs, intentions, positive patterns and actions, you'll find you are energized by what you do even in the middle of the challenges and crises you have to face.

Positive actions you resonate with have an effortless and energizing quality to them. They are often a joy to accomplish. With this level of coherence, you may be surprised to find yourself smiling through a project at midnight!

## POSITIVE ACTION IN ACTION

In this activity, you select action steps that strengthen the new pattern you created in the Compensation Repatterning mini-session—the activity you did at the end of Key 7: Repatterning (p. 124).

Read again the coherent statement you selected. Here's a list of specific actions to amplify the frequency of your intention. Tune in to your felt sense to find the one or ones that strengthen your new neural pathway.

### Specific action to amplify your resonance with your coherent statement

- Read your statement out loud and pay attention to its

thought, image, feeling, and the sound of the words. Do this at least once a day for three days or more.

- Stand with your arms slightly outstretched, palms turned upward, and tone aloud a "haa" sound as you exhale. Repeat several times during the day to reinforce your resonance with unconditional love at your heart center.

- Smile for five minutes every day for three days.

- Mend something you care about and enjoy using it or wearing it.

- Fuel your intention with positive images of the outcome you are aiming for and the actions leading to that outcome. (Athletes who visualize their movements and the outcomes they want set more records than those who only work out.)

- Spend at least five minutes a day sitting still, in silence, with a straight spine. Enjoy the inner calm that comes from relaxing deeply.

- Tell a friend, family member or staff member what you appreciate about them.

## Strategic action to create positive change

- If your goal is about bringing more love into your life, host a gathering of friends and ask everyone to bring a poem about love to read aloud.

- Register for a class that will give you the knowledge you need to manifest your goal.
- Plan a one-day vacation, pick the date and do what would bring joy to your heart. (Ignore the voice that gives you all the reasons you can't.)
- Do one completely new and loving action for yourself and/or for someone else for 1–7 days.
- Ask yourself "What action do I need to do right now that will create positive change?"

By acting with conscious positive intention, you are connecting to the unified field of unconditional love at just the frequency you need.

## HIGHLIGHTS

▲ Coherent actions and intentions are two aspects of one equation. They are mutually supportive.

▲ The energy exchange between your coherent action and the unified field creates a magnetic field of attraction.

▲ No matter how small the coherent action, it is highly significant.

▲ Muscle checking enables you to identify the action that reinforces your resonance with the frequency of your coherent outcome.

▲ Consistent and coherent action over time strengthens the unconscious neural pathways that empower new behaviors, responses and outcomes.

▲ *Spontaneous coherent actions* occur when you experience new behaviors and perceptions after a shift in your resonance, free of all effort on your part.

▲ *Specific coherent actions* identified by muscle checking reinforce your new neural pathways, even when the actions appear to be unrelated to what came up in your session.

▲ *Strategic coherent actions* identified by muscle checking are specific tasks that directly relate to your session and actively move you toward positive change and your goals.

▲ Because of your resonance with coherent action, the action feels effortless, recharges you and gives you a sense of joy, no matter how hard you may need to work to achieve your goal.

~~~

# QUANTUM CHANGE

*Quantum change is not something*

*that happens outside ourselves;*

*it happens inside ourselves.*

*The non-linear nature of quantum change*

*means that a tiny input of energy*

*can create a huge change.*

*Anything is possible.*

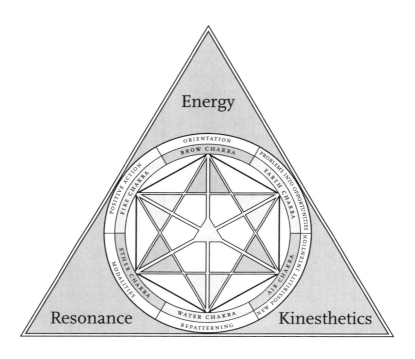

Energy

Resonance

Kinesthetics

ORIENTATION

BROW CHAKRA

PROBLEMS INTO OPPORTUNITIES

POSITIVE ACTION

FIRE CHAKRA

EARTH CHAKRA

NEW POSSIBILITY INTENTION

ETHER CHAKRA

AIR CHAKRA

MODALITIES

WATER CHAKRA

REPATTERNING

# QUANTUM CHANGE

~~~

*A human being is a part of the whole, called by us*

*"Universe," a part limited in time and space.*

*He experiences his thoughts and feelings as something*

*separate from the rest—a kind of optical delusion*

*of his consciousness. This delusion is a kind of prison*

*for us, restricting us to our personal desires*

*and to affection for a few persons nearest to us.*

*Our task must be to free ourselves from this prison*

*by widening our circle of compassion*

*to embrace all living creatures*

*and the whole of nature in its beauty.*

ALBERT EINSTEIN

In India last year a friend asked me, "Why quantum? That's as small as you can get. Why do you want to focus all your efforts on the tiny world of quantum change?"

She asked a great question, one that goes to the heart of my purpose for this book and all that I teach. In new physics, a quantum is considered an infinitely small and indivisible unit of neutral energy. So what could this tiny parcel of energy possibly have to do with transformation, self-healing and achieving the best of who we really are?

I focus on quantum change not because of the small size of the world at this level, but because of what lies beyond the level of vibrating subatomic particles: the primal divine energy of sound and light that inspires us on our upward and inward journey of self-healing in all areas of our life. When Lao Tzu writes that a journey of a thousand miles begins with the first step, he is describing the process of quantum change. Every step, whether a thought, word, intention or action, organizes particles at the quantum level and makes us receptive to spirit. Each succeeding step on our journey attracts more energy, which leads to quantum leaps that carry us way beyond our original expectations.

## Quantum behavior

How does this happen? As science describes it, quantum change is a vivid moment when randomly moving subatomic particles suddenly, inexplicably, come together in a new and orderly alignment. This new and orderly alignment is initiated when we heed Lao Tzu's encouragement to take the first step, Gandhi's urging to become the change we seek, and Martin Luther King's eloquent encouragement to realize the dream.

I focus on quantum change because it happens, not on the outside, but first on the inside. Consciousness—the field—is the hidden initiator that leads to all positive change. It is the point at which a stuck-in-a-rut state of mind suddenly shifts into an open flow of energy, focus and positive action. It represents a new order and alignment that impacts every aspect of our being. Quantum change isn't linear, left-brained or logical.

One minute we may feel stuck in anxiety, and the next minute we are giving the best presentation of our lives. We have jumped into a new and orderly alignment of our natural abilities.

Quantum change is built into the structure of the universe. We saw it with the spinning electron changing its direction and the related electron thousands of miles away instantly responding. Once a first step is taken, there is an instant response somewhere else. The result may show up as a small personal change or as dramatic cultural change.

Quantum change leads to events that may be described as the tipping point, the critical mass, the hundredth monkey, the Butterfly Effect. By whatever name or theory we call it, each new event begins with the power of one person resonating with coherent thoughts, words, intentions and actions. The resulting change may appear full blown within a culture: the rapid spread of email worldwide, the popularity of yoga in the West, the blossoming of computer services in the East.

I continue to focus on quantum change because it integrates consciousness, mind, emotions, body, and all life experiences in an upward spiral of hope. It gives me pleasure knowing there are scientific premises that support the inspirational teachings found in all spiritual traditions, and that there are scientific underpinnings to everything I now teach. We might, as scientific theory says, begin at the level of the very small, like the movement of a butterfly's wing, and yet create an exponential effect around the globe.

## The collective question

Quantum change is a way to address the challenges we now face in our lives. Expressing worldwide concerns, the astrophysicist Steven Hawking posed a question at Yahoo Answers for internet users to ponder: **In a world that is in chaos politically, socially and environmentally, how can the human race sustain another 100 years?**

When you read this question, your first reaction may, like mine, be a sense of overwhelm. Then I remember that each one of us has the capacity, by one means or another, to invite quantum change into our lives. By applying universal principles like the Nine Keys and by taking coherent steps, we can all—individually or at the level of societies and governments—provide resolution to the collective issues raised in Steven Hawking's question.

KEY 1: ENERGY    It is the radiant energy of light and sound that sustains life. Our ability to recognize when our personal energy is out of balance, along with our ability to restore our energy to its balanced flow, brings the possibility of hopeful change to our political, social and environmental systems as well.

KEY 2: RESONANCE    We are vibrating energy beings living in a field of vibrating frequencies. The frequencies we resonate with create a field of attraction that determine what we experience. Therefore personal and global evolution depend on attuning ourselves to ever more coherent frequency bandwidths in the unified field.

KEY 3: KINESTHETICS    We are wired for success and survival. Through Resonance Kinesiology, we have the ability to find and transform the non-coherent static that interrupts our reception of life energy. We can also identify the coherent frequencies we need and move into resonance with them in order to enhance the flow of our energy. This process is true for individuals as well as for global organizations.

KEY 4: ORIENTATION    When we are oriented toward our spiritual ideals, we are able to thrive in any situation. We have an inner compass that keeps us on track toward personal and collective nurturance, unity, truth and heart connection.

KEY 5: PROBLEMS   Rather than resisting a problem and being disturbed by its distressing static, we benefit by resonating with the opportunity it contains. Evolution, both personal and organizational, comes when we resonate with meeting the coherent needs underlying the problems of the individual, group or nation.

KEY 6: INTENTION   Nothing beneficial happens without coherent, positive intention. When we resonate with intentions and the needs that underlie our intentions, we move easily through the inevitable obstacles that arise. We then become receptive to quantum leap solutions and transformation, both personal and global.

KEY 7: PATTERNS   Rather than superimposing our non-coherent patterns on our relationships and our world, we need to create and resonate with coherent patterns. Our goal is to access the higher frequencies of consciousness where attitudes and perceptions shift and our experience of inner and outer reality changes for the better.

KEY 8: MODALITIES  Any modality is a coherent energy input that creates a sense of well-being. Modalities, when used in association with an intention, a problem or pattern, have the power to transform our resonance with destructive patterns and bring us into resonance with constructive patterns. Modalities facilitate the moment when subatomic particles suddenly align to create a new, more ordered pattern, which potentially brings balance to the global body-mind system.

KEY 9: ACTION  Every action, whether non-coherent or coherent, attracts more of the same. This is how we are bound to the consequences of our actions. When we resonate with high-frequency intentions and the coherent actions that bring them to fruition, we become radiant, magnetic vehicles for quantum change and conscious living.

## Hope

The most positive and far reaching change happens when we resonate with the highest frequencies within ourselves. Whether we follow the path of the Tao, the Kalima, the Shabd, the Logos, the Great Spirit or the Holy Spirit, conscious living ultimately involves resonating with the highest of frequencies within ourselves and going into action to manifest them in our daily lives.

This is the quality of conscious living that the great spiritual beings radiate simply by their presence in the world. Each one of us, by living consciously, has the capacity to become attuned to higher frequencies within ourselves, so we bring the beauty of our compassion to every person we touch—with a look, a word, a moment shared.

When we live the nine principles described in this book, we enter the world of conscious living. We no longer need to stay in a downward spiral of upset and distress. Through our resonance with the highest frequencies within, we do more than just sustain ourselves. **We thrive, innovate, develop, grow and live our very best, through meaningful action and service, in all that we do.**

~~~~

# THE RESONANCE
# REPATTERNING® SYSTEM

After reading this book and doing some of the modalities, you may be wondering what it would be like to experience a session for yourself, or to do a session on yourself or someone close to you.

If your curiosity has been piqued, the best place to start is with one or more sessions with a Certified Practitioner of the Resonance Repatterning® system.

If you decide you want to do sessions on yourself or on others, one of the many benefits of receiving sessions is that it makes it easier for you to learn Resonance Repatterning.

## Finding a practitioner

You can always find a practitioner via the internet. Both www.ResonanceRepatterning.net and www.holographic.org link you to a list of Certified Practitioners, arranged by state and country.

If you don't have a computer available, you can call the Holographic Repatterning Association at 1-800-685-2811 for names and numbers of Certified Practitioners.

Don't worry if there isn't a practitioner in your immediate neighborhood. Many practitioners work equally well with you by phone as they do in person, and some practitioners are experienced in doing distance sessions by proxy.

According to new physics, we are all vibrating fields of energy and inseparably linked through the unified field. This means that practitioners are able, with your verbal permission, to access your frequencies through muscle checking for the purpose of giving you a session. Proxy sessions do not use psychic abilities or powers. The practitioner simply does the distance session on your behalf, muscle checking from the six Keys on the Mandala for what you need.

You'll receive feedback and follow-up, along with positive action steps. Proxy sessions are also useful, when done with the person's permission, for children, the elderly, someone who is in a coma or in hospital, and with animals.

## Finding a seminar

The Resonance Repatterning training teaches you all the transformative protocols, how to muscle check on yourself and others, how to do all the modalities, and how to give sessions to yourself—and, if you wish, to others.

Seminars and teachers are listed at www.ResonanceRepatterning.net. You can also call 1-800-929-1787 for more information, and sign up at the website for a monthly newsletter that includes upcoming seminar schedules.

When you register online for a seminar, you'll be contacted directly by the teacher or seminar coordinator, or you can phone a teacher or the seminar coordinator. Seminars are generally scheduled over the weekend, and last two to three days. Seminars are also taught as intensives.

# RESONANCE REPATTERNING
# AT A GLANCE

## The System

The Resonance Repatterning® system, based on the Nine Keys, facilitates personal transformation, self-healing, and achieving the best of who you are. Almost anyone can learn this system regardless of their background or training.

## The Idea

We are energy beings living in an ocean of energy frequencies. Our quality of life is determined by the frequencies we resonate with. We can consciously change the frequencies we resonate with and change our experience of life through the Resonance Repatterning® system.

## The Innovations

- **The Resonance Repatterning system** is an integrated, practical, energy-based method that provides the means for putting into action, in daily life, theories from the human potential movement and new physics.

- **More than seventy-five Repatterning protocols** are documented in training manuals, facilitating easy access by students and practitioners. They include statements that reflect a full range of coherent and non-coherent frequency patterns for resonance transformation.

- **Resonance Kinesiology** (the Resonance Repatterning muscle checking system), based on a precise theory of muscle checking, accesses information from the body-mind to identify and transform the frequencies we resonate with.

- **A worldwide range of modalities** is compiled in a readily accessible format in the Resonance Repatterning manuals. The modalities are used for transforming resonance patterns in a Resonance Repatterning session and can also be applied in a practical and beneficial way in the home and work setting.

- **The Energy Constriction Release** is a powerful process modality for in-depth relief when an unconscious, highly charged emotional memory manifests as discharging (usually anger or tears) or disembodying (a disconnection from present reality).

- **A universal application**, Resonance Repatterning can be applied in any human activity for the achievement of greater coherence and well-being: for improved health, relationships, career and business performance; in education, athletics, and creative activities; and for the proliferation of coherent patterns in global organizations and political systems.

## Resonance eStore

The products needed for Modalities and some of the Positive Actions are available at the Resonance eStore, along with books, CDs and other helpful materials:

www.ResonanceRepatterning.net/store/

## Holographic Repatterning® Association

The Resonance Repatterning system was originally known as Holographic Repatterning. Certified Practitioners are members of the Holographic Repatterning Association, an independent, incorporated, member-operated certifying body affiliated with the Resonance Repatterning Institute. For more information about the Association, its practitioners, and scheduled events:

www.holographic.org

## Free Monthly Newsletter

For the latest news about Resonance Repatterning theories, research, and seminars, sign up for a monthly newsletter at:

www.ResonanceRepatterning.net

# WORDS WE USE

**applied kinesiology**   Originally, the strength and weakness of a muscle was used by medical doctors and physical therapists to determine the presence of nerve impulses to a specific muscle. Dr. John Thie, who developed the Touch for Health system, departed from the original use of muscle strength, using it instead as an indicator of under- or over-energy (too much or too little) in each of the twelve acupuncture meridian channels. This muscle checking system is called *Applied Kinesiology*, and is now a generic term for the field of using muscle strength as an indicator for gaining information about the body-mind system.

**attraction**   A magnetic field that pulls one object toward another.

**body-mind**   The body, emotions and mind are different frequencies of an individual's energy system, stepped down from the highest frequency of the eternal soul or spirit to the slower frequencies that sustain the human body, emotions and mind. It is often referred to as the body-mind system, the body-mind field or the biofield. When vibrating harmoniously, all the frequencies combine to create each person's unique signature frequency, which creates resonance, or not, with others.

**chakras**   Lit. 'wheels' in Hindi; according to the 5,000-year-old Indian Ayurvedic healing tradition, the seven major chakras are spinning energy reservoirs that step down high-frequency source energy in sequence from the crown reservoir to the reservoir at the base of the spine. This energy powers our physical body and all its functions. At subtle levels the state of our chakras determines every thought and feeling we have, our physical well-being, how we relate to others and what we achieve. Like electricity, which scientists do not fully understand yet can see its effects and use its power, so with the chakras: we may not understand what they are or be able to measure their high-voltage frequencies, but we can see the effects in the state of our physical, emotional and mental well-being.

**coherence**   A state of order and harmony where things hold together and form a unified whole; its opposite is chaos or non-coherence. A higher state of coherence is always preceded by chaos. In Chaos Theory, within the chaos the new coherent pattern is present and ready to emerge.

**coherence muscle check**   In the Resonance Repatterning system, the practitioner muscle checks for information on what creates a higher energy state of coherence, using what Resonance Repatterning calls the coherence muscle check. Coherence muscle checking is not used to determine what is true or false. This muscle check simply provides information about which choice makes our system more coherent, based on the range of choices we have available. *See also* **Coherence Continuum, p. 5; resonance muscle check; Key 3: Resonance Kinesiology**

**consciousness**   Known as the witness self, the observer or soul. Soul, or consciousness, is who we are and is a drop in the ocean of pure Consciousness. The soul, which animates the body-mind system, is conscious, eternal, and one with the Divine. Without soul or consciousness, the mind, feelings and body are inert. *See also* **energy**

**cue**   A statement, coherent or non-coherent, used as a prompt when muscle checking.

**divine nature**   This is who we are, free of personality and limiting patterns; also called the authentic self, the soul, spirit or consciousness.

**energy**   The essential life force that imbues and maintains all of creation. We exist as a coalescence of energy frequencies, living in a field of pulsing frequencies. New physics proves that life is not just a chemical reaction, but a wave of energy out of which the particle of physical matter materializes. At the body-mind level, energy is known in different cultures as *chi, ki, prana* or *ether.* Beyond the body-mind level, some of the names for the primal energy that creates and sustains all dimensions of life are the Holy Spirit, the Logos (Word), the Shabd (Sound or Word), the Kalima (Word), the Tao (the reality of the undefinable Supreme) and Consciousness. *See also* **Key 1: Energy**

**entrainment**   A state of synchronization when a stronger frequency, or oscillation, brings other frequencies that are close by into alignment with it. For example, a large pendulum clock synchronizes the swing of smaller pendulum clocks when they are all placed together on a wall. Entrainment or synchronization with coherent or non-coherent frequency pulsations can lead to outcomes that support, or do not support, the well-being of the individual, family or nation.

**felt sense**   Your automatic body and feeling response to your thoughts and outside events. You become aware of your felt sense by paying attention to how you are reacting physically and emotionally at any moment in time. *See also* **inner knowing; neurotransmitters**

**field**   The backdrop for all of existence, the field or unified field is the primal divine energy that creates and sustains everything in the creation. The field is an ocean of pulsing frequencies of energy—of which we are a part and within which we all live, breathe and experience our perception of reality. Through this field we are connected to everything in the creation. Einstein believed "the field is the only reality." *See also* **unified field; Key 1: Energy**

**frequency**   The infinite number of pulsations, oscillations or cycles per second that all dimensions of life radiate within the field—whether rocks, trees, thoughts, feelings, brainwaves, sound, color, or the soul.

**general muscle check**   The name given in Resonance Repatterning to the most general level of the resonance muscle check; used for checking the frequencies of the body-mind system as a whole. *See also* **resonance muscle check; Key 3: The Kinesthetic Sense**

**harmonics**   Any musical note has an automatic series of related harmonic notes. When we listen to a person trained in harmonic overtoning or when a singing bowl is struck, we can hear these harmonic notes. The fundamental note being sounded, the harmonic overtones themselves and the intervals between them are known to be effective for resolving tension and stress and for creating harmony in the body-mind field.

**holographic**   A state in which each part contains the whole. Cut a holographic picture or hologram into ten pieces and shine a light through each one and you will see the original, whole, three-dimensional picture in each of the ten pieces. All beings—parts of the hologram—are indivisibly a part of the whole.

**Holographic Repatterning®**   The original name for the Resonance Repatterning® system. The name Holographic Repatterning was based on the concept that we are holographic. Like a hologram, we consist of overlapping frequencies, we are indivisible, and the database of everything that has ever occurred to us is stored as frequencies in our body-mind system. Each one of us is a microcosm of the whole, a miniature cosmos that contains the entire creation within it, including the Source of all. Michael Talbott, author of *The Holographic Universe*, says "we are holographic shards in a holographic universe."

**holographic storage**   The holographic nature of the body-mind field potentially allows us to access frequency information wherever it is stored in the universal hologram or the unified field. Because we are holographic and indivisible, when we change the part, we change the whole. For example, the ear is a microcosm of the whole body; massaging the ears or receiving aural acupuncture therefore balances vibrating energy flows throughout the whole body-mind. Similarly, when we change our personal resonance for the better, we set in motion a balancing flow of energy for us, and holographically, for all others.

**imprint**   A pattern of frequencies, consisting of images, feelings, beliefs, perceptions and actions that you resonate with. The imprint becomes reinforced over time by activating the same response and its corresponding neural pathway. Any remotely similar situation tends to reactivate the same response, imprinting the life-depleting or life-supporting frequency pattern more and more deeply. Through Resonance Repatterning we change our resonance with life-depleting imprints and resonate instead with life-supporting imprints. *See also* **Key 7: Repatterning**

**inner knowing**   The kinesthetic sense, the fifth sense of feeling and touch, is associated in Resonance Repatterning with the quality of inner knowing of frequencies. The kinesthetic sense is our physiological inner knowing to which we connect through our felt sense and the muscle checking response. This inner knowing of frequencies, communicated through our body and muscle responses, enables us to be aware in any situation of what is coherent and life-enhancing for us and what is non-coherent and life-depleting for us. The kinesthetic sense of inner knowing of frequencies has supported our survival as a species for millions of years. *See also* **kinesthetic sense**

**kinesiology**   The physiological study of muscles and movement, specifically the on/off response to pressure on a muscle indicating the presence of nerve impulses. In the Resonance Repatterning system, the on/off muscle response is a reflex response to electrical impulses transmitted via the autonomic nervous system in response to a cue. *See also* **Resonance Kinesiology; Key 3: The Kinesthetic Sense**

**kinesthetic sense**   In Resonance Repatterning, the fifth sense is not just feeling and touch, but includes body-mind awareness of the frequencies of thoughts, emotions and everything in our environment. Feelings, touch, movement and gut responses are the organs of the kinesthetic sense, in the same way that the eyes are the organs for seeing.

Responses to everything we feel, consciously and unconsciously, are transmitted as electrical impulses by the nervous system to the brain, body and muscular system. The vast majority of these responses are unconscious but can be picked up through muscle checking and the felt sense. *See also* **felt sense; muscle checking**

**kinesthetics**   In Resonance Repatterning, kinesthetics is considered to be the principle of inner knowing through the felt sense and the muscle response to all the energy frequencies within ourselves, in our environment and in the unified field that our body-mind resonates with. *See also* **Key 3: The Kinesthetic Sense**

**living matrix**   *See* **unified field**

**mandala**   A circular geometric design symbolizing the universe. In the Resonance Repatterning system, six of the Keys and their relationship to six of the chakras are represented in a mandala formation. The Resonance Repatterning Mandala, designed by Chloe Faith Wordsworth, is a pictorial representation of the complete methodology for creating quantum change; it is the means by which Resonance Repatterning practitioners access the information represented by each of the Keys in order to give an integrated, in-depth session. The Mandala can be seen on p. 2.

The tetrahedron at the center, where all the lines of the Mandala cross, represents the pivotal hub where integration for quantum change is initiated. *See also* **The Nine Keys**

**meridians**   In the ancient Chinese healing system, acupuncture meridians are known as the Officials of the Kingdom. The twelve officials maintain harmony in the body-mind system for physical health and longevity as well as for emotional and mental well-being. On the physical level these meridians are energy channels associated with specific organs and functions. Harmonizing the flow of life energy or chi through the meridian channels maintains the vitality of the body-mind system as well as the vitality of our relationships, organizations, communities and nations.

**modality**   Any healing action that creates greater coherence in the physical, emotional and mental field. In Resonance Repatterning a modality is used to input energy into the body-mind system. The Resonance Repatterning seminars teach practitioners a broad range of modalities based on ancient and modern healing traditions from around the world, including modalities in the categories of sound, color and light, breath, movement, fragrance, energetic contacts and processes specific to the Resonance Repatterning system developed by Chloe Faith Wordsworth. *See also* **Key 8: Modalities**

**muscle checking**   In the Resonance Repatterning system, muscle checking is a form of biofeedback based on the strong/relaxed response of muscles to messages from the autonomic nervous system, which in turn is responding to frequency inputs from the body's kinesthetic sense. In a Resonance Repatterning session, muscle checking is used for gaining information about resonance (resonance muscle check) and what creates a higher state of coherence (coherence muscle check) in the body-mind system. *See also* **Resonance Kinesiology; Key 3: The Kinesthetic Sense**

**neurotransmitters**   Neurotransmitters are biochemicals activated by the body-mind system in response to thoughts, feelings, physical needs and environmental cues; they relay, amplify and modulate electrical signals between neurons (nerve cells) and other cells. A cascade of neurotransmitters results in either a stressed or a relaxed response. The neural pathways they create become fixed by our repetitive perceptions, beliefs and actions.

**non-coherence**   A state of disorder also known as incoherence, de-coherence or chaos. In Chaos Theory it is said that within the chaos the new ordered pattern is already present and ready to emerge. A state of chaos always precedes greater coherence.

**patterns**   At the macro level, consistent patterns can be seen in nature — in the curves and spirals of the human body and in the movements of water, wind, sand, plants and galaxies. At the micro or personal level, patterns are formed in the body-mind frequency field according to our responses to each experience. *See also* **Key 7: Repatterning**

**perception**   An internal point of view about reality that does not necessarily describe external reality. According to the pioneering work done by molecular biologist Bruce Lipton, the way we perceive an event — rather than the reality of the event itself — activates our DNA and causes our cells to move toward growth and expansion or to constrict for the sake of safety, which means that no growth is possible. Therefore when we change our non-coherent perceptions, we are empowered at the cellular level to expand and grow toward our fullest potential.

**point of choice**   At any moment in time we have a choice to spiral up to a higher energy state of greater coherence or to stay in the lower energy state of non-coherence, experienced as problems and difficulties. In the Resonance Repatterning system, the point of choice is the eternally present moment for coming into greater alignment with consciousness. Coming to the point of choice allows us to use our energy in a positive way, to resonate with what is life-enhancing and to become more aware, through our kinesthetic sense, of what supports higher states of coherence for our body-mind well-being. *See also* **Key 5: Problems into Opportunities; Quantum Change**

**quantum leap**   This term is used in quantum physics to mean any unexpected change from one energy state to another, with no transition between the two states. In the simple act of heating water, electrons become excited and cause the temperature to increase in unpredictable leaps rather than in a smooth linear progression.

**repatterning**   In the Resonance Repatterning system, everything we do is designed to neutralize or cancel our resonance with life-depleting frequency patterns and strengthen or amplify our resonance with life-supporting frequency patterns. This is known as repatterning. The Key of Repatterning is designed to identify and transform specific patterns developed by Chloe Faith Wordsworth. In the Resonance Repatterning system, there are more than seventy-five of these universal patterns that Chloe formulated into coherent and non-coherent cues. *See also* **Key 7: Repatterning**

**resonance**   Through the natural phenomenon of resonance, one pulsating frequency sets similar frequencies vibrating, just as striking one tuning fork automatically sets the second tuning fork of the same note vibrating too. Resonance leads to an energy exchange between the two tuning forks. This shows that objects with the same frequency resonate with each other, even at a distance, as seen with the spin of partnered electrons and the transmission of radio frequencies through outer space.

When anything is in resonance, it vibrates with a frequency that is natural to it and is most easily sustained by it. Resonance Repatterning facilitates the individual or organization to vibrate at the resonant frequency that is natural to it and most easily supports a state of well-being.

In the Resonance Repatterning system, the principle of resonance provides the foundation for quantum change. *See also* **Foreword; Key 2: Resonance; Key 9: Action**

**resonance muscle check**   Unique to the Resonance Repatterning system, the resonance muscle check is the particular form of muscle checking used to confirm what we do or do not resonate with. Through the Resonance Repatterning system, we are able to identify the non-coherent patterns we resonate with that cause our problems, and the coherent patterns we need to resonate with that lead to transformation. *See also* **coherence muscle check; Key 3: The Kinesthetic Sense**

**Resonance Kinesiology**   A name to describe the theory-based muscle checking system that is unique to Resonance Repatterning. In Resonance Repatterning the practitioner muscle checks for information on what creates coherence (using the coherence muscle check) and also muscle checks to confirm what we do or do not resonate with (using the resonance muscle check).

There are three levels used with the resonance muscle check: the general muscle check (checking the body-mind system as a whole); the specific muscle check (checking a specific organ, meridian, chakra or other particular part of the body-mind system); and the umbilical muscle check (used when positive frequency patterns have been cancelled out).

The Resonance Repatterning muscle checking system is taught in easy steps during the Resonance Repatterning seminars. *See also* **The Nine Keys; Key 2: Resonance; Key 3: The Kinesthetic Sense**

**specific muscle check**   Unique to the Resonance Repatterning muscle checking system, the specific muscle check is used when the frequency of a specific organ, meridian, chakra, age, level or other particular part of the body-mind system is holding the negative resonance. *See also* **general muscle check; Key 3: The Kinesthetic Sense**

**spirit level**   "Spirit" here does not refer to the soul; it is a Five Element Acupuncture term referring to a state of deep resignation that blocks the self-healing process. By working at the "spirit level," the client's vision and hope are renewed so they can benefit from whatever self-healing system is being used. Muscle checking allows the Resonance Repatterning practitioner to find out precisely what is needed to resolve the spirit level resonance.

**tetrahedron**   A tetrahedron is a platonic solid formed of four three-sided triangles. In the Resonance Repatterning system, the tetrahedron is found in the center of the Coherence Continuum and the Mandala.

Its three base points represent body, emotions and mind; its central three-dimensional point represents spirit or consciousness.

**umbilical muscle check**    Unique to the Resonance Repatterning muscle checking system, the umbilical muscle check is used when positive frequency patterns have been cancelled out or neutralized, and there is "zero" energy for what is life-enhancing. When a baby or child entrains with patterns that directly oppose what is life-enhancing, then life-supporting frequencies are cancelled. This manifests as an umbilical muscle response. *See also* **resonance muscle check; Key 3: The Kinesthetic Sense**

**unconditional love**    Unconditional love in this book refers to a flowing, harmonious response to ourselves, to others and to the Divine, regardless of outside circumstances. Love is who we are at the core of our being. All transformative, spiritual and self-healing processes ultimately lead to more profound levels of love: love of the essential self, which unfolds as self-realization and realization of the Divine within.

**unified field**    A term used in physics to describe the infinitely coherent and abundant field that unifies the various forces of nature. Called a "spin network" or "quantum plenum" by some physicists, the unified field is the fabric that interconnects all particles in the universe. In this context, the unified field is the web of radiant forces extending through supposedly "empty" space. *See also* **field**

# REFERENCES AND
# FURTHER READING

Bentov, Itzhak. *Stalking the Wild Pendulum*. Rochester: Destiny Books, 1977.

Brian, Denis. *Einstein, A Life*. New York: John Wiley & Sons, 1996.

Connelly, Dianne M., PhD. *Traditional Acupuncture: The Law of the Five Elements*. Laurel (Maryland): Tai Sophia Institute, 1994.

Cook, Theodore Andrea. *The Curves of Life*. New York: Dover Publications, 1979.

Dennison, Paul E., PhD, and Gail Dennison. *Brain Gym*. Ventura: Edu-Kinesthetics, Inc., 1986.

Diamond, John, MD. *Your Body Doesn't Lie*. New York: Warner Books, 1979.

Dossey, Larry, MD. *Reinventing Medicine*. New York: HarperCollins, 1999.

Dyer, Wayne. *There's a Spiritual Solution to Every Problem*. New York: HarperCollins, 2002.

Gardner, Kay. *Sounding the Inner Landscape: Music as Medicine*. Maine: Caduceus Publications, 1990.

Gerber, Richard, MD. *Vibrational Medicine: New Choices for Healing Ourselves*. New Mexico: Bear & Company, 1988.

Gladwell, Malcolm. *The Tipping Point*. New York: Little, Brown and Company, 2002.

Goleman, Daniel, Annie McKee and Richard E. Boyatzis. *Primal Leadership: Learning to Lead with Emotional Intelligence*. Boston: Harvard Business School Press, 2004.

Gray, Alex. *Sacred Mirrors: The Visionary Art of Alex Gray*. Vermont: Inner Traditions, 1990.

Hale, Theresa. *Breathing Free: The 5-Day Breathing Programme that Will Change Your Life*. London: Hodder & Stoughton, 1999.

Hanna, Thomas. *Somatics: Reawakening the Mind's Control of Movement, Flexibility, and Health*. Cambridge (Massachusetts): Da Capo Press, 1988.

Hellinger, Bert, with Gunthard Weber and Hunter Beaumont. *Love's Hidden Symmetry: What Makes Love Work in Relationships*. Phoenix: Zeig, Tucker & Co., 1998.

Hines, Brian. *God's Whisper, Creation's Thunder: Echoes of Ultimate Reality in the New Physics*. Threshold Books, 1995.

Hunt, Valerie V. *Infinite Mind: The Science of Human Vibrations*. Malibu: Malibu Publishing, 1995.

Jenny, Hans, PhD. *Cymatics: A Study of Wave Phenomena*. 2 vols. Epping (London): Macromedia Press, 2001.

Judith, Anodea. *Chakra: Wheels of Life*. Ottowa: Laurier Books/Jaico, 2004.

Kerin, Dorothy. *The Living Touch*. London: Courier Printing & Publishing, 1949.

Laszlo, Ervin. *Science and the Akashic Field*. Rochester: Inner Traditions, 2004.

Leonard, George. *The Silent Pulse*. New York: EP Dutton, 1978.

Lipton, Bruce, PhD. *The Biology of Belief: Unleashing the Power of Consciousness, Matter and Miracles*. Santa Rosa: Elite Books, 2005.

McCarty, Wendy Anne, PhD. *Welcoming Consciousness: Supporting Babies' Wholeness from the Beginning of Life*. Santa Barbara: Wondrous Beginnings Publishing, 2006.

McTaggart, Lynn. *The Field: The Quest for the Secret Force of the Universe*. New York: HarperCollins, 2002.

Oschman, James L., PhD. *Energy Medicine: The Scientific Basis*. London: Harcourt Publishers, 2000.

Pearce, Joseph Chilton. *The Biology of Transcendence*. Vermont: Park Street Press, 2002.

Pert, Candace B. *Molecules of Emotion*. New York: Scribner, 1997.

Purce, Jill. *The Mystic Spiral*. New York: Thames and Hudson, Inc., 1990.

Radin, Dean. *Entangled Minds: Extrasensory Experiences in a Quantum Reality*. New York: Paraview Pocket Books, 2006.

Rosenberg, Marshall B., PhD. *Nonviolent Communication: A Language of Life*. Encinitas: Puddle Dancer Press, 2003.

Selzer, Richard, MD. *Mortal Lessons: Notes on the Art of Surgery*. New York: Harcourt, 1996.

Somé, Malidoma. *Of Water and the Spirit*. New York: Penguin, 1995.

Stone, Randolph, DC, DO. *Polarity Therapy*. Reno: CRCS Publications, 1986.

Talbott, Michael. *The Holographic Universe*. New York: HarperCollins, 1992.

Wolf, Fred Alan. *Taking the Quantum Leap*. New York: Harper and Row, 1981.

Worsley, J.R. *Classical Five Element Acupuncture: The Five Elements and the Officials.* New Mexico: Redwing Book Co., 1998.

Zohar, Danah and Ian Marshall. *Who's Afraid of Schrodinger's Cat?* New York: Harper Perennial, 1998.

_____. *Spiritual Capital: Wealth We Can Live By.* San Francisco: Berrett-Koehler Publishers, 2004.

# ACKNOWLEDGEMENTS

This book is the culmination of thirty-five years of training, practicing and teaching in the complementary healthcare field. I am profoundly grateful to all those who have touched my life and made the writing of this book a physical reality:

- The teachers I have had in the field of alternative health-care, who imparted their wisdom and knowledge so generously: Dr. Randolph Stone, who developed Polarity Therapy; Professor J. R. Worsley and the teachers at the Traditional Acupuncture Institute (Tai Sophia in Maryland); Sharry Edwards for her gift in developing Signature Sound Works; Dr. Paul Dennison, founder of Educational Kinesi-ology; Patti Steurer, who developed the Balance format; and all the other teachers I studied with, too many to name.

- My clients, who loved the synthesis of modalities I brought to their sessions and gave their time and trust so that I could find their underlying patterns. Everything I developed, and therefore this book, came out of those early years of exploration and excitement.

- The students of the Resonance Repatterning® system (which was previously known as Holographic Repattern-ing®), who continuously pushed me to my growing edge to write the system down, develop it, recreate it, improve the teaching of it—and in the process, myself as well.

- My friends and family, with whom I shared my early ideas, and whose presence, intelligence and sensitive responses further inspired the development of the

Resonance Repatterning system: Karine Bourcart, Anthea Guinness, Lindis Guinness, Dorinda Hartson, Ardis Ozborn, Shady Sirotkin, Tom Stone, and I am sure many more.

- The teachers of the Resonance Repatterning system, whose belief in this method and whose desire to teach it made this book a necessity. Extra thanks to Ardis Ozborn and Mary Camaris for being the impetus that initiated the writing of this book.

- My sister Lindis Guinness, whose five years of unstinting help in the early days gave me the time to develop the system, write the manuals and teach.

- The readers of various drafts of *Quantum Change Made Easy*—for their enthusiastic responses and helpful suggestions: Josie Airns, Joel Bennett, Yvonne Bost Brown, Chris Cameris, Sandy deGroot, Michael Fisher, Mandira Gazal, Sarah Gibbons, Bruce Glanville, Anthea Guinness, Al Harris, Naomi Kronlokken, Bobbie Martin, Georgia Miles, Ardis Ozborn, Netta Pfeifer, Liz Tobin, Carolyn Winter and Kristin Zhivago.

- The practitioners, teachers and clients whose personal experiences with Resonance Repatterning added heart to the ideas shared in this book, including Catalina Abril, Meryl Chodosh-Weiss, Michael Fisher, Gail Glanville, Ardis Ozborn, Cynthea Paul, Tim Reeves, Kimberly Rex and Cheri Stewardson.

- Carla ElDorado, who for many years has devoted her energy to preparing the seminar manuals and their graphics and illustrations for printing, which paved the way for the writing of this book.

- Karine Bourcart for bringing Resonance Repatterning to Mexico, Latin America and Spain, for overseeing the translation of the seminar manuals into Spanish, for training students and teachers, and for her continued dedication to maintaining the high values the Resonance Repatterning system represents.

- Jim Oschman, for graciously agreeing to write the book's Foreword and so clearly articulating the science behind the concepts of resonance, coherence and quantum leaps.

- I wrote this book only through the help of Gail Noble Glanville. I was constantly energized by her joy and total involvement from the initial stages of the very first booklet draft to the finished product—including the dialogues that clarified the concepts of kinesthetics and muscle checking for both of us. I deeply appreciate her ability to keep the whole project moving forward; for the ease and pleasure of working together as a team in the seemingly endless process of writing, re-writing, editing, re-editing, adding and deleting. I shall be ever grateful for the gifts Gail brought that made the outcome of this book a reality!

- Profound appreciation to Anthea Guinness, whose professional editing and proofreading brought this book to a level it would not otherwise have achieved. By questioning, clarifying, organizing, improving the text, and asking for stories, she helped us transform the book from beginning to end.

- My parents, John and Karis Guinness, for all their many gifts in who they were and what they gave to so many. It is my hope that this book and my life will honor them and their memory.

- Gratitude beyond words to my spiritual teacher, whose "rose petal heart of compassion" is my inspiration and whose teachings challenge me daily to become aware of and ultimately understand the radiant, unified field of the Tao, the Shabd, the Logos—the highest and best within myself.

CFW
March 2007
Scottsdale, Arizona

# ABOUT THE AUTHORS

CHLOE FAITH WORDSWORTH — founder, practitioner and teacher — created the Resonance Repatterning system for quantum change. With more than thirty-five years of experience in the complementary healthcare field, Chloe has spent the last fifteen years refining and teaching Resonance Repatterning, as well as developing new seminars and writing manuals for practitioners. Along with the certified teachers of Resonance Repatterning, Chloe has taught the system to thousands of people around the world.

GAIL NOBLE GLANVILLE — author and corporate coach — is presently the managing director of the Resonance Repatterning Institute and a long-time Certified Practitioner of the Resonance Repatterning system. She lives in Jamestown, RI.

CONTACT — info@ResonanceRepatterning.net.
1 800 929 1787